A Guide to
Koh Samui and Environs

Dan Reid

**Photographs by
Alberto Cassio**

ASIA BOOKS

Published and distributed by Asia Books Co. Ltd.
5 Sukhumvit Rd., Soi 61
Bangkok 10110, Thailand
P. O. Box 40
Tel. 391-2680, 392-0910
Fax. (662) 381-1621, 391-2277

All photographs by Alberto Cassio

Edited by Dolores Ciardelli

Designed by Christopher C. Burt

Typeset by COMSET Limited Partnership

Map artwork by Winnie Sung

Produced by Twin Age Ltd., Hong Kong

Printed in Hong Kong

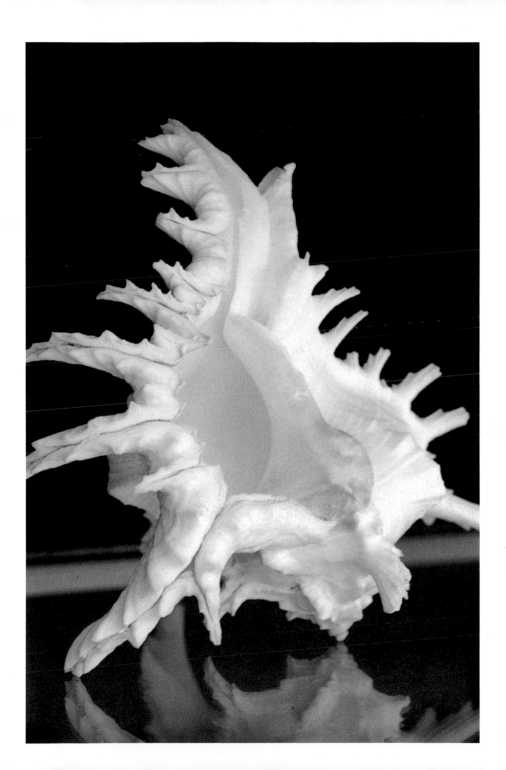

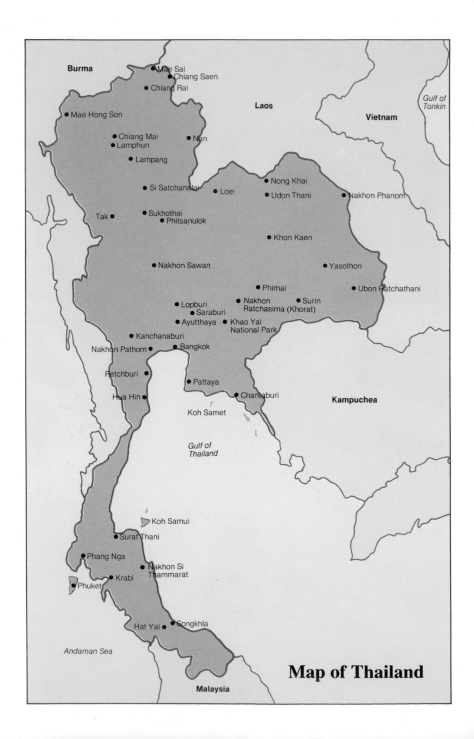

Burma

Mae Sai
Chiang Saen
Chiang Rai

Laos

Gulf of
Tonkin

Mae Hong Son

Vietnam

Chiang Mai
Lamphun
Nan

Lampang

Si Satchanalai
Loei
Nong Khai
Udon Thani
Nakhon Phanom

Tak
Sukhothai
Phitsanulok

Khon Kaen

Nakhon Sawan
Yasothon

Phimai
Ubon Ratchathani

Lopburi
Nakhon
Ratchasima (Khorat)
Surin
Saraburi
Ayutthaya
Khao Yai
National Park

Kanchanaburi

Nakhon Pathom
Bangkok

Petchburi

Pattaya

Hua Hin
Chantaburi

Kampuchea

Koh Samet

Gulf of
Thailand

Koh Samui

Surat Thani

Phang Nga

Nakhon Si
Thammarat
Krabi

Phuket

Hat Yai
Songkhla

Andaman Sea

Map of Thailand

Malaysia

ACCESS ROUTES TO THE ISLANDS

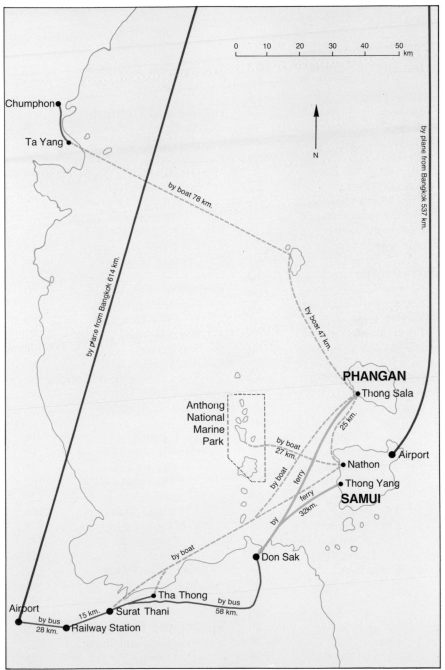

Contents

KOH SAMUI

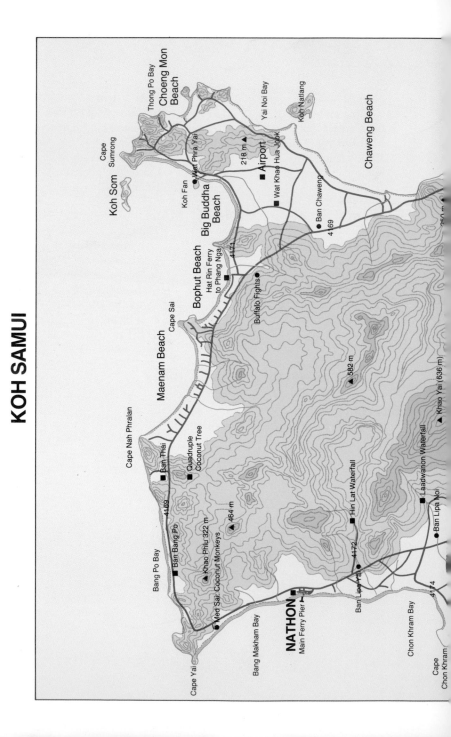

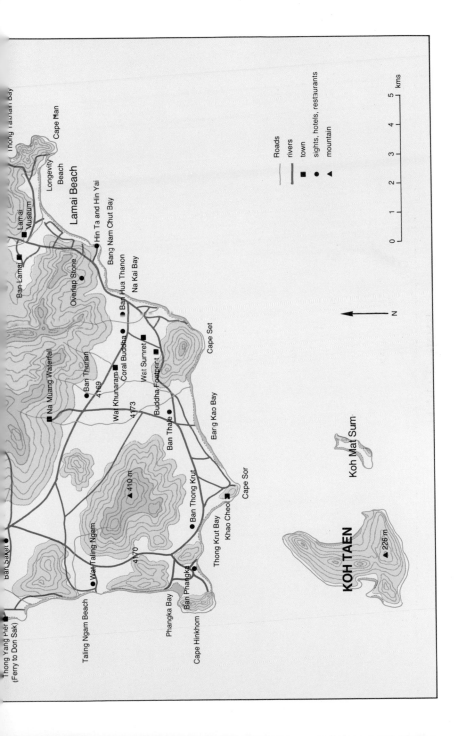

Thong Yang Pier
(Ferry to Don Sak)

Ban Saket

Taling Ngam Beach

Wat Taling Ngam

Phangka Bay

Ban Phangka

Cape Hinkhom

Thong Krut Bay

Khao Cheol

Cape Sor

Barg Kao Bay

Ban Thong Krut

▲ 410 m

Ban Thae

4170

4173

Buddha Footprint

Wat Khunaram

Coral Buddha ●

Wat Sumret ■

Ban Thurian ■

4169

Na Muang Waterfall ■

Overlap Stone ●

Ban Lamai ■

Lamai Museum ■

Longevity Beach

Cape Man

Thong Ta-nan Bay

Lamai Beach

Hin Ta and Hin Yai ●

Bang Nam Chut Bay

Na Kai Bay

Ban Hua Thanon ●

Cape Set

KOH TAEN

▲ 226 m

Koh Mat Sum

N

Roads

rivers

■ town

● sights, hotels, restaurants

▲ mountain

0   1   2   3   4   5   kms

Idyllic Isle of Samui

Like so many other idyllic seaside sanctuaries in Asia from Goa to Bali, Samui was first discovered by footloose hippies and shoestring backpackers in the early 1970s, and for over a decade it remained their secret hideaway. In those days, a thatched A-frame hut without electricity or running water was regarded as heaven-on-earth, all for about a dollar a night. Today you can still find such bargain bungalows on some of Samui's more remote capes and coves, but they're becoming more and more scarce. Many of the original pioneers of Goa and Bali have already moved over to neighboring Koh Phangan and Koh Tao.

With the advent of regular passenger and vehicle ferry service from Surat Thani on the mainland, and the more recent opening of an airport with daily flights from Bangkok, Koh Samui ("Samui Island") has joined the ranks of international island resorts. There are now about 240 hotel and bungalow facilities scattered along the island's beautiful beaches and bays, ranging in price from 40 to 7,000 baht (US$1.60-$280) a night, with an additional 124 facilities on nearby Koh Phangan and about two dozen on Koh Tao.

Much to everyone's surprise, however, this recent flurry of development has not spoiled Samui's idyllic ambiance—at least not yet—and there are reassuring signs that local authorities intend to prevent the sort of wretched excess that has all but ruined many of the resort beaches around Pattaya and Phuket. Somehow Samui has managed to absorb the sudden boom in its tour and travel trade without losing its native charm, and with only a few eyesore exceptions, most of the new resort facilities have been tastefully designed to harmonize with rather than dominate the natural environment. High-rise construction is forbidden, and beach-front development is strictly controlled.

Koh Samui is different and diverse—an island with a niche for every taste and budget. For well-heeled jet-setters, the Samui archipelago is rapidly becoming the Caribbean of Asia—a quick and convenient getaway with all the deluxe trimmings. For hipsters on the lam in Asia, Koh Samui, Phangan, and Tao have become the latter day heirs to the hallowed traditions engendered long ago in Goa and Bali. The island is endowed with such an incredibly rich variety of beaches and bays, capes and coves, that it seems like a dozen different islands rolled into one. You can loll in limpid lagoons or surf in frothy breakers, snooze on white sand beaches or snorkel in clear coral reefed bays. You can snack on grilled prawns and enjoy a soothing alfresco massage on the popular beaches of Chaweng and Lamai, or stake out your own private sand castle on Big Buddha Beach or Bang Po Bay. Never will you feel crowded or cornered, and nowhere will you be more than a short stroll from a palm-fringed bar or snack shack.

Despite the current spate of resort development, a remarkable sense of peace still prevails on Koh Samui. People are happy to be there—residents and travelers alike—and no one seems in a hurry to leave. Indeed, judging from the chronic no-shows on departing boats and planes, leaving Koh Samui can be quite difficult. The place clings to you and makes you wish to stay longer—like waking up in a comfortable bed with a lissome lover. Who wants to get up and go back to work when another perfect day is smiling at the door?

Fortunately, Samui lies far enough away from Bangkok and other big cities to discourage day trippers from littering its shores. It's not the sort of place to go for a day or two of packaged fun. It takes at least a couple of days just to wind down to the island's tranquil pace and start enjoying its soporific serenity. One doesn't go to visit Koh Samui: one goes to live there, even if only for a week or two.

Getting There

It used to take a full day and night to get to Koh Samui from Bangkok, but with the opening of the airport in 1988, you can now get there in just over an hour. Still, for landlubbers and budget travelers, the old land and sea routes remain quite popular.

By Ferry There are three ferry piers along the Surat Thani coast on the mainland and two on Koh Samui, serviced by two rival ferry companies. Which one you take depends on how you get to Surat Thani from Bangkok (bus or train) or which ferry company the travel agent you use represents.

Vehicle Ferry Samui Ferry Co. operates the vehicle and passenger ferries from the Don Sak Pier (located 60 km –38–miles from Surat Thani), to the Thong Yang Pier on Koh Samui, about 10 km (6 miles) south of the main town of Nathon. This is the ferry you'll usually end up taking when you purchase 'packaged in Bangkok' train and bus tickets that include the ferry crossing to Samui. The ferry departs Don Sak daily at 8:00 am, 10:00 am, 2:00 pm, and 5:00 pm, the fare is 40 baht per passenger, and the crossing takes 1 1/2 hours. For a motorcycle and driver the fare is 70 baht, for a car and driver it's 180 baht, plus 40 baht for each additional passenger in the car. The bus ride from Surat Thani Bus Station out to Don Sak Pier takes 45 minutes to an hour and costs 10 baht. From Surat Thani Train Station it takes one to 1 1/2 hours and costs 20 baht to reach the Don Sak Pier. From Samui's Thong Yang Pier back to Don Sak, there are five daily departures at 7:30 am, 10:00 am, 12:00 noon, 2:00 pm, and 4:00 pm.

Express Passenger Ferry Songserm Travel operates the express passenger ferries from the Tha Thong Pier (6 km –4 miles–from Surat Thani) directly to the pier in Nathon, Samui's main town. The fare is 90 baht per passenger and the crossing takes about two hours, with three daily departures at 7:30 am,

12:00 noon, and 2:30 pm, November through May, and two departures at 7:30 am and 12:30 pm June through October.

From Nathon Pier back to Surat Thani there are three daily departures at 7:15 am, 12:00 noon, and 3:00 pm, November through May, and two departures at 7:30 am and 3:00 pm, June through October. The return run from Samui includes a bus ride to the train station, for a total fare of 110 baht.

Night Ferry Songserm Travel also operates a slow night boat from Ban Don Pier in downtown Surat Thani to Koh Samui, departing at 11:00 pm nightly and reaching the Nathon Pier around 5:00 am. The fare is 60 baht for upper deck berth (pillow and mattress) and 30 baht for lower deck (straw mat). This lower deck service must resemble the hold of old slave boats with a four foot ceiling and passengers packed in like sardines—not recommended for claustrophobics or during rough weather. The return night run from Nathon back to Ban Don departs Samui at 9:00 pm and arrives around 3:00 am. This route is a convenient last resort if you miss the last express or vehicle ferry in the afternoon, but otherwise it's not the preferred way to go.

If your destination is Koh Phangan and you wish to skip Koh Samui, there's also a nightly ferry from Ban Don Pier direct to Koh Phangan, departing at 11:00 pm and arriving around 6:00 am next morning. Upper deck fare is 80 baht, lower deck is 50 baht.

High Speed Jumbo Ferry In early 1991, Navakun Transport Co. inaugurated a High Speed Jumbo Ferry service from Bangkok's Chao Phya River directly to Koh Samui, departing around 7:00 pm and arriving around 8:00 am next morning. The ferry is a large, luxurious cruising vessel with dining room and bar, private cabins, and other amenities. Unfortunately, the ferries have been plagued by engine trouble, resulting in more cancellations than departures, but Navakun Transport is trying to solve these mechanical problems and institute regular service. This is a relaxing, hassle-free way of getting to Samui, if you like boats. To check if this service is available, telephone Navakun Transport in Bangkok at 398-1170/2 or their agent, Thai Overlander, at 258-4778/80 or 258-9246/7.

By Bus An express air-conditioned bus ride between Bangkok and Surat Thani takes about 10 hours and costs 225-300 baht, depending on the size of the bus, with seven departures daily in both directions. Ordinary buses run 18 times per day, the ride takes 12-13 hours, and the fare is 130 baht. There is also 'ordinary' daily bus service between Surat Thani and Phuket (61 baht, 6 hours), Krabi (45 baht, 4 1/2 hours), and Hat Yai (67 baht, 3 hours). Special air-conditioned minibus service to and from all of these points is also available by prior reservation through travel agents in Samui. The cost for this service from Samui to Phuket is 190 baht.

If you're coming from or going to Bangkok by bus, the best way is to book a ticket straight through to or from Koh Samui which includes the vehicle ferry from Don Sak. The all-inclusive fare to or from Nathon is 250-350 baht and may be readily purchased through tour bus companies or any travel agent in Bangkok or Samui. From Samui, direct bus service to Bangkok departs daily at 1:30 pm from the Bus Station located 1 km south of Nathon on Route 4169. Ordinary buses are 143 baht, a/c buses with food service run 258 baht, and a/c buses without food service cost 204 baht. The above prices do not include an extra 40 baht ferry fare. Similar package deals are available between Samui and Phuket, Krabi, and Hat Yai.

By Train The State Railway of Thailand operates four daily Rapid Trains (11 1/2 hours) and four daily Express Trains (9-11 hours) between Bangkok and Surat Thani. From Bangkok, you can purchase railway tickets which include the bus ride to the Don Sak ferry pier and the ferry crossing to Koh Samui. This only costs you 30-50 baht more than making the bus and ferry connections yourself, and it's well worth the time and trouble it saves you in Surat Thani.

Rapid and Express train fares from Bangkok, inclusive of bus and ferry connections, run about 400-480 baht for second class sleeper berth with fan, 500-530 baht for second class sleeper with a/c, and about 800 baht for a first class a/c sleeper cabin. Second class seats run about 285 baht, third class seats 210 baht. Due to the long ride, the best way to go is by second class sleeper on an evening train, which arrives in Surat Thani around dawn and gets you out to Koh Samui by noon. First class sleeper on the train is not really worth the extra expense, since the cabins are usually freezing cold from excessive air-conditioning. Second class sleeper berths are clean and comfortable, and the food and beverage services are quite sufficient.

(following page) Storm clouds gather over Maenam Beach. Samui's rainy season is July through October.

19

By Air Koh Samui's new airport is one of the most attractive air facilities in Southeast Asia and recently won an award for its original design. It also has a very good gift shop with beautiful batiks and local coconut shell handicrafts.

Bangkok Airways operates five daily flights from Bangkok to Samui at 7:30 am, 10:30 am, 11:00 am, 1:30 pm, and 4:00 pm. Return flights to Bangkok depart Samui daily at 9:00 am, 12:00 noon, 2:30 pm, 3:00 pm, and 5:30 pm. One-way fare is 1,880 baht, and the flight time is 1 hour and 10 minutes. Bangkok Airways flies three types of aircraft on this route: Dash 8-300 (56 seats), Dash 8-100 (37 seats), and Banderante (18 seats).

There is also one daily flight from Phuket to Samui at 1:35 pm, and from Samui to Phuket at 12:30 pm. One-way fare is 1,100 baht and flight time is 40 minutes.

The runway at Samui Airport will soon be extended to accommodate Boeing 737 jets in anticipation of rapidly growing arrivals from Bangkok and possibly international destinations as well.

Koh Samui's attractive new airport won an award for its original design.

22

Longtail boats can be hired for short hops or day trips. Judge the condition of the boat and the appearance of the boatman before handing over any money.

Travel Advisory

Climate and Clothing Prime time weather-wise in Koh Samui is from February through June, when the sky is generally clear and the sea calm. From July through October it rains on and off, although the rain rarely falls for more than a few hours at a time. Many people find the rainy season quite refreshing, it cools the island and leaves the air crisp and clear. Often it rains on one side of the island, while the other side basks under sunny skies.

From April through September, southwest winds blow huge thunder clouds across the island at night, producing marvelous electric light shows in the sky. August and September are the second most popular months to be in Koh Samui, February to June being the most popular. From October through January, Koh Samui is subject to occasional heavy winds and rains. This is the least crowded time of year and good bargains on bungalows can be made during this off-season period.

Average temperatures throughout the year range between 25-35 degrees C (76-95 degrees F).

Koh Samui's balmy tropical climate and abundant vegetation make it an ideal habitat for mosquitos, although they are usually only a nuisance at night. A variety of good mosquito repellents are available at shops throughout the island, including an effective roll-on based on aromatic plant oils. Most bungalows provide mosquito nets upon request.

Attire on Koh Samui is decidedly casual by day as well as night. Light, loose, comfortable clothing such as shorts, sandals, and T-shirts are acceptable attire in restaurants and hotels, but not in temples. If you decide to visit some of the island's temples, be sure to wear long pants and a proper shirt. It's also a good idea to wear a hat and sun glasses during mid-day hours to protect skin and eyes from the strong tropical sun. 100% cotton clothing is by far the best choice of material in tropical climates.

Nude sunbathing and swimming is definitely not appropriate in Koh Samui, for it violates Thai etiquette and embarrasses Thai people. Topless sunbathing for women is all right on some of the island's private resort beaches and on the more remote beaches of Koh Phangan and Koh Tao, but it is not recommended on Koh Samui's main public beaches.

Local Transportation The main mode of public transport in Koh Samui is by covered pick-up trucks converted into taxis, called *songtaos*. Fleets of *songtaos* ply Samui's main circle-island road all day long until about 9:00 pm at night. Simply hail them down as they pass by. The fare from Nathon to Maenam, Bophut, and Lamai is 15 baht, 20 baht to Big Buddha, Choeng Mon, and Chaweng. The same fares prevail from the Thong Yang Pier south of Nathon. Note that *songtaos* do not cover the steep headland road between Chaweng and Lamai. They go from Nathon to Chaweng and all points in

The main mode of public transportation is covered pick-up trucks called songtaos, *which ply Samui's main circle-island road all day. Just hail them down - they'll squeeze you in!*

between via the road's northern loop and Nathon to Lamai via the southern loop. Occasionally you may encounter a surly *songtao* driver who'll try to charge you more if he thinks he can get away with it. Just pay him the standard fare and be on your way.

From the Nathon Pier there is a regular air-conditioned minibus service to Samui Airport six times daily for 40 baht. There are also two daily a/c buses to Surat Thani Airport for 150 baht (including the ferry), two a/c buses to Surat Thani Bus Station for 80 baht (including ferry), and five ordinary buses to Surat Thani Bus Station for 60 baht (including ferry).

There are many motorcycle rental agencies in Nathon and elsewhere on Samui which rent motor bikes and jeeps by the day. The going rate for a 125 cc motorbike is 150 baht/day, but you can often negotiate a lower rate for long-term rentals. Larger motorcycles run about 400 baht/day, and jeeps go for 600-900 baht, depending on the model. Many bungalows also have small fleets of motorbikes and a few jeeps for rent to their guests.

Some of the bigger, more reliable motor rental agencies in Samui include "Siam Jeep" and "Home Ad" in Nathon, "Dan" in Maenam, "World Motor Rental" in Bophut, and "Iron Shark" in Lamai. When renting a motorbike, be sure to take it out for a spin first to make sure the brakes, gears, steering, and other mechanisms work properly, and always wear a helmet.

Motorcycling on Koh Samui and Koh Phangan

From experience and the increasing number of signs proclaiming "Wounds Dressing" popping up around the islands a word of caution seems to be appropriate.

Koh Samui

Most roads are surfaced on Koh Samui with asphalt and there is no real need to risk injury on your holiday with a motorcycle. Large vehicles commonly drive straight at you and push you off the road. Always give way. If you must have a bike choose the smallest one, with four gears but no clutch. They are usually reliable, light, stable and easy to turn around.

The fancy, heavy, and powerful jobs are unstable and treacherous. To climb up and off the machine is already an achievement.

Koh Phangan

Here motorcycling is almost a must. At the moment there are no jeep rentals available and most of the trails around the island are passable by foot or motorcycle only.

The road conditions vary from poor to dreadful and in some cases not even a motorbike will get you to where you want to go. If you never rode a bike before, forget it and get around by boat. If you feel up to the task choose a machine with wide tires and a powerful engine. Stay away from the 125 cc water cooled variety. Roads can suddenly become very steep, scarred by rain gullies into which you inevitably get trapped and thrown off your machine. When climbing and the road suddenly gets steep and rough, proceed in your lowest gear with the maximum possible speed, don't get frightened half way up a hill, but keep your momentum; if you are too timid and the engine dies the bike suddenly seems to weigh tons and you cannot hold it from sliding back. Brakes become useless and you will have to let it fall over, possibly burning your leg on the smoldering exhaust pipe, a burn the outcome. Your feet can be in the way as well and a bloody mess will keep you wondering about your wisdom for the months ahead.

Always wear jeans, and shoes with socks. Swimming trunks and flip flops are a sure ticket to the hospital.

If you get burned or wounded go straight to a doctor. Ironically motorcycles are sometimes rented out by joint venture drug stores cum rental agencies, so they potentially double their money on each rental. Tropical climates and sea water infect wounds very quickly and a scratch may develop into a major infection in no time.

There is a paved road that runs completely around the island, Route 4169, with a lower branch looping along the southwest corner, Route 4170, and another branch, Route 4171, looping between Big Buddha and Choeng Mon in the northeast corner. Smaller unpaved roads branch off the main roads giving access to some of the island's more remote beaches and inland areas.

Although the main roads are paved, they are very narrow and not always well maintained. Even more hazardous than the road itself is the local style of driving, which includes passing on blind curves, tail-gating, speeding, and other dare-devil stunts. By no means should foreign visitors participate in such motor madness. Every year a dozen or more visitors to Koh Samui lose their lives or limbs in horrible traffic accidents that turn dreamy holidays into bloody nightmares. If you're going to drive on Samui, especially on a motorbike, drive defensively and with great caution.

Communication Except for the large resort hotels and some of the bigger bungalows, most hostels in Samui do not have private telephone lines. Those that do charge about 25 baht per minute for calls or faxes to Bangkok, and a lot more for overseas calls. There are plenty of places in Nathon and elsewhere around the island that offer overseas telephone service, just look for the "Overseas Tel & Fax" signs over their doors.

You can also make long distance calls and post letters and packages at the main Post Office in Nathon, located about 200 meters north of Nathon Pier.

The telephone area code for Thailand is 66, Koh Samui is 077, and Bangkok is 02. If you wish to telephone or fax any of the local Samui telephone numbers listed in this book from overseas, dial 6677 plus the number. To phone Bangkok from abroad, dial 662 plus the number. To call Samui from Bangkok or elsewhere around Thailand, dial 077 plus the local number.

Accommodation Koh Samui offers a wide range of choice in accommodations, from tiny thatch huts for 40 baht/night to huge deluxe suites at fancy resorts for up to 7,000 baht/night. Virtually every beach and bay on the island now has some sort of hostel facility, and more are being built every year. The current count in Samui is about 240 facilities, ranging from small 6-8 hut bungalows with out-house toilets and communal showers to big five-star resorts operated by Bangkok-based hotel chains.

There are several factors to consider when selecting a bungalow or hotel in Koh Samui. One is price, which usually reflects the standard of facilities and services offered. All the major beaches and bays have simple, inexpensive facilities to choose from, but only a few have the big, international-class resorts favored by the wealthy jet-set.

Another perhaps more important consideration is ambiance. If you want to be close to the action—such as shops, restaurants, bars, night life, and beach bunnies—pick a place on Chaweng or Lamai. If you prefer a more quiet, private ambiance with plenty of local color, you'll be happier on Bophut, Maenam, or Big Buddha. And if it's complete solitude you're looking for, try some of the quiet capes and coves on the southern and western shores, or perhaps move off-island to Koh Phangan or Koh Tao. Wherever you stay on Samui, it's always easy to get to any other part of the island by *songtao* or rented motor vehicles.

Generally, the smaller family-run bungalow operations offer the most friendly feeling, personal hospitality, and authentic local flavor. The big chain-operated resorts tend to go overboard on luxury and expense and conform to a standard pattern of service not much different from similar operations in Hawaii, the Caribbean, and other tropical destinations. On the other hand, if it's pampered luxury with all the frills you're looking for and cost is no object, then perhaps the big resorts are for you.

With such a great variety to choose from, there's no need to commit yourself to one place for your entire stay. Pick a place that seems to suit your requirements for the first few nights, then explore the island for other alternatives and move elsewhere if you find something that suits you better.

During the months of February, March, April, and August, space can be quite tight, and it's therefore a good idea to book a room well in advance. During the rest of the year it's a buyer's market, and you can often negotiate substantial discounts at many places.

In the section on "Places," a recommended selection of bungalows on each beach and bay is mentioned and briefly described, with a more complete list of names and addresses provided at the end of the book in the "Travel Directory."

Koh Samui offers a wide range of accommodations, from tiny thatched huts to huge deluxe suites.

Island Profile

History Koh Samui was first settled by fishermen plying the waters of the Gulf of Thailand (Siam) about 1,500 years ago. These early settlers discovered fertile fishing grounds around the islands and ample protection from high winds in the coves along the northern shores of Maenam and Bophut, where the earliest fishing communities were established. Fishing has remained one of the island's economic mainstays ever since.

Koh Samui also appears as part of "the known world" on ancient Chinese maps dating from the late Ming Dynasty (16th century AD), indicating an active maritime trade with China. Samui may well have been part of the extensive trade network established at that time by the famous Chinese eunuch-admiral Cheng Ho. Chinese ceramics discovered in sunken ships off Samui's shores lend further evidence to this early trade connection with China.

During World War II, Japanese military forces attempted a brief occupation of the island, but they quickly abandoned the scheme and left when angry local fishermen killed a group of them for encroaching on their precious fishing grounds.

Although Koh Samui is now part of Thailand's Surat Thani province, the island has traditionally remained somewhat aloof from the rest of Thailand, distinguished by its own distinctive local culture and ethnic pride. For almost two centuries it remained virtually unknown to the Western world, and even Thais from the mainland rarely ventured there. Around 1971, it was finally "discovered" by intrepid Thai and foreign travelers, who hitched rides to Samui on coconut boats. It wasn't until the mid-1980s that Koh Samui's charms became generally known to mainstream tour and travel operators who put the island on the map of international itineraries and thereby inaugurated Samui's modern history as a tropical holiday resort.

Geography Koh Samui is part of an 80-island archipelago in the southern waters of the Gulf of Thailand, located 35 km (22 miles) off the Surat Thani coast and 710 km (443 miles) south of Bangkok. With an area of 247 sq. km (37 sq. miles), it's Thailand's third largest island and the largest of the seven inhabited islands in this group. The others are Koh Phangan (12 km –8 miles– north of Samui), Koh Tao (60 km –37 miles–north), Koh Taen (2 km off the southwest cape), Koh Ta Loy, Koh Ma Ko, and Koh Ta Pao. 30 km (19 miles) northwest of Samui lie the exotically scenic limestone islands of Anthong National Marine Park.

Two-thirds of Koh Samui consists of steep densely foliated mountains, with the highest peak (Khao Yai) located in the center of the island at 636 meters (2,100 feet). Swift flowing streams irrigate the island, and there are several scenic inland waterfalls.

Coconut palms blanket the entire island from the beaches right up to the mountain peaks, and these, in addition to fishing, form the backbone of the local economy, with an average two million coconuts shipped to Bangkok every month. The rich nutty aroma of coconuts being roasted over open fires for copra production is one of the pleasant sensory pleasures of Samui, Phangan, and the Tao islands.

In addition to coconuts, Koh Samui grows the notoriously odiferous but famously delicious durian, the exotic bristly pink rambutan, as well as a variety of bananas, papayas, and mangos. Samui shares a distinction with Goa and Phuket of being one of the few places on earth that cultivates cashews as a cash crop. The cashew nut grows from a bell-shaped fruit that resembles a rose apple. This fruit is sweet and can be eaten when ripe, but do not attempt to peel and eat the green nut, which exudes a caustic oil and must be handled with care. Processed cashews are available at shops and restaurants all over the island, plain or roasted.

On the subject of geography, you will no doubt notice huge raw gashes scarring the mountain sides around the island, where the earth has been clawed away and twisted trees left broken like match sticks. These eyesores, which are visible for miles offshore, look like battle grounds where Godzilla and King Kong fought to the finish, but in fact these wounds are inflicted on the island by commercial developers, who pay local landowners for the right to excavate the earth as landfill for their various construction schemes, much to the dismay of local residents and environment-conscious travelers.

Samui is one of the few places on earth that cultivates cashews as a cash crop. The cashew nut grows from the bottom of a bell-shaped fruit, which is sweet and can be eaten when ripe.

32

Smiling is an important form of communication in Thailand! Most chao samui
(Samui folks) remain genuinely gracious and open-hearted people.

People The inhabitants of Koh Samui number about 35,000 and refer to themselves as *chao samui* ("Samui folks") rather than *chao thai* as elsewhere in Thailand, indicating the pride they take in their local culture and ethnic identity. Although excessive exposure to the foibles of the tourist trade has jaded some of these "Samui folks," such as *songtao* drivers and a few Nathon shopkeepers, most of them remain genuinely gracious and open-hearted people. Like most islanders, *chao samui* are also quite crafty when it comes to doing business, as anyone who's attempted

joint ventures there can testify. This also means that bargaining is de rigueur in most shops and virtually all market stalls, as well as for negotiating good off season discounts at family-run bungalows.

Lifestyle and Etiquette Despite the laid-back, informal lifestyle which makes sojourns on Koh Samui so pleasant and relaxing, there are some basic rules of etiquette which foreign visitors should observe in order to avoid offending local sensibilities. Nudity in public places, for example, offends most Thais and should be avoided, except perhaps on strictly private beaches. Many Thai women are so conservative about exposing their bodies in public that they go swimming fully clothed in blouses and pants, a common sight in Samui.

When invited into a private home in Koh Samui always take off your shoes at the door. When visiting temples, do not wear shorts and skimpy T-shirts, and be sure to leave your shoes at the door when entering shrine halls.

Anger will get you nowhere in Samui, or anywhere else in Thailand for that matter. This is one of the most difficult lessons for hot-headed *farangs* (foreigners) to learn. The best approach to even the most frustrating problem is a smile and patient dialogue. The key Thai phrase here is *chai-yen*, which literally translates as "cool heart" and means, "Have patience!" The Thais remain cool as cucumbers even under heavy fire, and farangs who wish to feel welcome here should learn to do the same.

It's no accident that Thailand is known as "The Land of Smiles," and Koh Samui is definitely "The Isle of Smiles." Smiling is an important form of communication in Thailand, and a well-turned smile will always get you a lot further than a frown, even when you're upset or angry.

Beyond these few basic guidelines, life in Samui is as easy-going and relaxed as can be, and *chao samui* are remarkably tolerant of even the oddest eccentricities. They partake fully of the fundamental Thai penchants for *sanuk* (fun) and *sabai* (comfort), and they enjoy sharing their pleasures with visitors from near and far.

Island Cuisine Koh Samui has a distinctive local cuisine based on the abundance of fresh seafood, fresh fruit, and the ubiquitous coconut. While basic Thai seasonings such as lemon grass, ginger root, coriander, and curry pastes are liberally used in cooking, the balance and blend in Samui are quite different from mainstream Thai cuisine. Coconut cream, for example, is applied more generously in local dishes than elsewhere in Thailand, giving Samui sauces and soups a smooth creamy texture and rich sweet flavor. Coconut cream is also the basis of local sweets and appears prominently in tropical cocktails and coolers, such as the famous *Pina Colada*.

There is a relatively small selection of fresh vegetables in Samui, so salads and vegetable dishes are not major features on local menus. Seafood, however, is always available in abundance, and is prepared with genuine gourmet flair. A brief guide to the delights of seafood in Samui appears in the chapter on "Seafood."

As elsewhere in Thailand, the presentation of food is an art in itself, as displayed here at the Wild Orchard Café on Chaweng Beach.

Fresh fruit is also abundant and inexpensive on Samui, and it forms the mainstay of island breakfasts. Bananas, pineapples, and papayas are available year around, while durian, rambutan, mangos, lychees, and other exotics come and go seasonally.

One of the greatest of all refreshments on a hot sunny day is the fresh milk of an ice-cold, green coconut sipped straight from the nut through a straw. You can then use a spoon to scrape out and eat the soft gelatinous meat inside. Not only is this a delicious libation, but coconut milk is also well known in traditional Thai as well as Chinese herbal medicine as a highly effective coolant to the blood and internal organs. It's often prescribed for fevers, headaches, colds, and stomachs overheated by excessive consumption of chili and alcohol. It's also a great way to nurse a morning hangover.

Thais enjoy deep-fried grasshoppers (takatain) *as a simple snack between meals, but tourists are unlikely to find this delicacy on their hotel menus.*

Sea Food

Next to coconuts, fishing has also traditionally been Koh Samui's economic mainstay, and seafood is as central to Samui's diet as beef in America or pork in China. Every restaurant and bungalow on the island serves fresh seafood, although the quality of what comes out of the kitchen varies widely from place to place, depending on the freshness of the fish and the talent at the stove.

By following a few basic guidelines, seafood gourmands should have no problem feeding their appetites for the fruits of the sea with maximum gourmet satisfaction:

1) Whenever possible, pick a restaurant that displays a fresh selection of the daily catch on iced counters by the entrance, then carefully select the freshest looking items.

2) Whenever ordering seafood at restaurants that don't have fresh displays, make it perfectly clear to the waiter that you're fussy about fish by pointedly asking if the fish (*plah*) is fresh (*sot*) today (*wan-nee*): *Wan-nee plah sot my*? (*my* indicates a question).

3) Generally, the more colorful a fish looks, the plainer it tastes. A lot of shallow water reef fish display beautiful rainbow colors, but their flesh often has poor taste and texture. Plain black, brown, yellow, and white fish generally taste best.

4) As a rule, it's best to specify that your fish be cooked by grilling (*yang*) or steaming (*neung*), in order to avoid any possibility of having it deep-fried in stale oil, which is a common preparatory stage of cooking in many Thai kitchens. Deep frying, especially in stale oil, is the best way to ruin the fresh flavor and texture of any seafood.

5) Ask around the bars and bungalows about the best places to eat seafood. Cooks come and go, and restaurants often change hands, but islanders always know where the freshest fish is served.

If you have any luck fishing while in Samui, take your catch to the kitchen of your bungalow or favorite restaurant and ask them to cook it for you in whatever manner you prefer. They'll charge you a small service fee for this, but the fish is free. You can also go to the fish market in Nathon or Hua Thanon at the crack of dawn to buy your own choice of the fresh morning catch, then have it cooked to your specifications later.

Grilling and steaming are the best ways for cooking seafood in Samui, but there are other ways. Braised with chili and garlic is a delicious Thai-Chinese method of cooking fish, but be sure to specify that they don't deep-fry the fish first. Menus always list this method as "Fried with Chili and Garlic," which should mean pan-fried and braised with chili and garlic but all too often means deep-fried then

ปลาทะเลของไทย

MARINE FISHES OF THAILAND

doused with chili and garlic.

Thai coconut cream curry is another good way of eating fresh seafood in Samui, especially prawns. For a spicy cold dish laced with shallots, coriander, lemon, and chilis, try a fresh seafood salad *yam talae*. Another marvelous Samui version of a traditional Thai dish is Shark in Coconut Cream Soup, a dish usually made with chicken.

Samui fishermen haul in all sorts of seafood in their nets and traps, among which the following varieties are most abundant:

Barracuda	Shark
Silver Pomfret	Rock Cod
Black Pomfret	Crab
Grouper	Lobster
Red Snapper	Prawns
Sea Bass	Shrimp
Perch	Squid

Reliable places for seafood on Chaweng are Madame Sim's, the Pig Sty, La Terrasse, Suan Kaew, and Poppies. In Nathon, you might try Sri Pornchai about 1/2 km north of town on Route 4169. In Maenam, the restaurant at Sea Fan turns out good fish dishes, and in Bophut you can count on savory seafood at Tid's and at Ziggy Stardust, which lays out an appetizing iced display of their fresh daily catch each evening.

But you don't have to go to a fancy restaurant to get good seafood in Samui, Phangan, or Tao: some of the simplest bungalows and seaside stalls prepare wonderful seafood, while some of the big expensive international resorts offer nothing but days-old frozen fish pretentiously presented, mundanely prepared, and over-priced. Simply follow the guidelines given above as well as your own instincts and you should have no trouble feasting on some of the finest seafood in Thailand.

Places on Koh Samui

Nathon
Located on the northwest side of the island, Nathon is Koh Samui's main town—actually it's the only town, the rest are villages—and usually it's simply referred to as "town." This is where the express and night ferries arrive and where all government agencies are located, including the Immigration Office, District Office, Police Station, and Post Office.

Nathon is an old-fashioned Southeast Asian island town, consisting mostly of weathered Chinese shophouses and open-air eateries, with a few modestly modern structures housing banks, travel agencies, and several supermarkets. But after a few weeks of beachcombing, especially out on Koh Phangan and Koh Tao, Nathon seems like the "Bright Lights, Big City."

Besides extending visas, banking, posting mail, and catching the bus or ferry back to Surat Thani, people come to Nathon mainly to shop and socialize. On the southern end of the main road, called **Taweeraj Pakdee**, you'll find a typical East Asian alfresco market selling all sorts of fresh produce, seafood, and pre-cooked dishes, as well as traditional Thai culinary ingredients and household accessories. The best time to browse this market is very early in the morning to find the freshest produce, but it stays open well into the afternoon as well. On this road you'll also find two modern supermarkets (Samui Mart and Giant), several drug stores, banks, and some express photo shops.

Running parallel to the main road but one block closer to the sea is narrow **Anthong Road**, a small lane featuring a variety of local handicraft and batik shops and a few restaurants, including the vegetarian **International**, which serves good tofuburgers and other veggy dishes at low prices. There are a number of interesting vendor stalls tucked into the alleys branching off Anthong Road selling locally produced handicrafts and ready made beachwear.

The third main street in town is the one which runs along the harbor, facing the sea. Here you'll find one of Samui's oldest hotels, the **Sea Side Palace**, where rooms go for 200-450 baht/night. Nearby is Songserm Travel, one of Samui's biggest travel agencies and the outfit that operates the express ferry from Nathon Pier. There are numerous open-front eateries on this street, where people hang out while waiting for buses or ferries. Try **Koh Kaew** for good home-style Thai food.

On the north end of the harbor road stands the Post Office, and across the street is an open *sala* (pavilion) where you can usually get a good, very inexpensive Thai massage, that is if all the masseurs aren't sound asleep having siestas.

One of the nicest shops in town is **Mook Rawai**, at 67/8 Taweeraj Pakdee Rd. They design and produce their own original line of silk-screen cotton T-shirts, and also sell traditional hand-woven apparel from northern Thailand, batik and handicrafts from Bali, and exotic beach and swim wear. At **Thonpho**,

NATHON

- Customs House
- Thai Boxing Stadium
- Chao Koh Hotel
- Hospital
- Immigration Ofc.
- Church
- Post Office
- Local Transport Station (for northern beaches and Chaweng)
- Police Station
- Na Amphoe Rd.
- Town Hall
- The Golden Lion

N

Harbor Rd.

Anthong Rd.

Taweeraj Pakdee Rd.

NATHON PIER (SERVICE TO SURAT THANI)

- Bus to Airport
- Food Stores
- Food Stores
- Bus Station (mainland points)
- Lighthouse
- Local Transport for Lamai Beach
- Thai Military Bank

GULF OF THAILAND

- Seaside Palace Hotel
- Bangkok Airways
- Market
- Thai Farmers Bank
- Tourist Police

roads (note arrows indicating one-way roads)

0   100   200
                        m

- Gas Station

44

Many vacationers on Koh Samui come into the town of Nathon to hang out and meet fellow travelers or to shop for traditional Thai handicrafts.

half a km south of town on the inland side of Route 4169, you'll find a variety of traditional Thai handicrafts for sale.

A lot of people simply come into Nathon once or twice a week to hang out and meet fellow travelers. One of the most popular watering holes for this purpose is **The Golden Lion**, located at the corner of Anthong and Na-Amphoe roads on the north side of town. The Golden Lion mixes great drinks and has a menu that offers tasty Thai as well as European dishes. A good place for sandwiches is **The Bird in Hand**, across the street and towards the harbor from the Golden Lion.

With all the cosy beach side bungalows around the island, there seems little point in staying in Nathon, but if that's where you prefer to be, try either the **Sea Side Palace** near the pier or the **Samui Bungalow** near the Post Office.

When you're ready to leave town, simply hop onto a *songtao* heading north towards Bophut, Big Buddha, and Chaweng, or south towards Lamai. They depart from the harbor street, near the massage pavilion, and they'll drop you off anywhere along the way around the island.

Beaches and Bays

The most popular beaches on Koh Samui are the "Big Six": Chaweng, Lamai, Maenam, Bophut, Big Buddha (*Phra Yai*), and Choeng Mon. But even the most remote coves and capes along the southern and western shores now have bungalow facilities, providing plenty of choice in ambiance and style as well as price.

The following guide to Samui's beaches and bays takes you clockwise around the island from Nathon, emphasizing the Big Six, but not neglecting the cosy coves and scenic capes along the way.

Bang Makham Bay As you head north on Route 4169 from Nathon, you'll see Bang Makham Bay to the west, with its extensive coral reef and rocky shore. This is not a good swimming beach, and only a few simple bungalow facilities may be found here. The main attractions are the **Garden Home Herbal Health Center** (see sidebar on Health Holidays for details) and a good Thai/Chinese seafood restaurant called **Sri Pornchai**, located about 1/2 km north of town in an attractive Thai-style house. At Cape Yai, where a lighthouse sits out on the point, the road veers east and heads into a small fishing village called Ban Bang Po (*ban* means "village").

Bang Po Bay This bay, which is fringed with extensive coral reefs, runs from Cape Yai eastward to the headland at Cape Na Phralan, about 15 km (9 miles) from Nathon. The beach here is fairly good during high tide, but not nearly as nice as those on the eastern side of the island. This is, however, one of the better bays for snorkeling, owing to its long shallow coral reef and calm waters. There's a pleasant, rather rustic bungalow facility midway along this beach called **Sun Beam** ensconced in a coconut grove far off the road. The cabins rent for 250-300 baht per night. If you come to Bang Po Bay for snorkeling, Sun Beam is a good place to start from.

Maenam Beach Continuing eastward, Route 4169 passes through Ban Maenam, a fairly large village with many shops, including diving and windsurfing centers and several small restaurants. This village services the two dozen bungalow facilities located further down along Maenam Beach. About a dozen narrow dirt roads branch off the main road towards the sea, giving access to the various resort and hostel facilities.

Maenam has a smooth white sand beach that stretches four km (2.5 miles) along a calm, scenic bay between Cape Na Phralan and Cape Sai, offering a clear view of Koh Phangan to the north. This is a good beach for swimming and sun bathing in a peaceful, quiet setting. Bungalows range in price from 50-2,600 baht. On the low-budget end of the scale, you might try **Friendly** or **Ubon**, where clean, simple huts go for 60-200 baht. For spacious, deluxe bungalows with a/c, fridge, and all the frills, a good bet is **Sea Fan**, which, for 2,500 baht/night also has a small swimming pool. The seaside restaurant at Sea Fan is one of the better places to eat in Maenam. A big, brash international resort and hotel complex called **Santi Buri** is under construction in Maenam, targeted at those interested in a big-budget, Club Med style vacation.

The Sea Fan boasts spacious, deluxe bungalows with all the frills, and its seaside restaurant is one of the better places to eat in Maenam Beach.

Bophut Beach Two km further east from Maenam Beach there's a sharp left turn off Route 4169 that takes you about 200 meters down to Bophut Village and Beach. Be sure to go straight toward the water after turning left, instead of veering off to the right onto Route 4171, which leads to Big Buddha Beach and the airport. When you reach the end of this small side-road, turn left and you're in Bophut. Ban Bophut is a quaint, quiet little fishing village and one of Samui's oldest settlements. The people here are particularly warm and friendly, and the whole place has an unhurried backwater ambiance that will appeal to those who seek peace and privacy while still remaining within easy reach of good food and transportation.

Bophut Beach is about two km (1.25 miles) long, with clean white sand and calm water. The ocean, especially near the village, is not as clear as Chaweng and Lamai, but if you stroll west toward Cape Sai you'll find good water for swimming. Due to the placidity of the bay here, Bophut is excellent for water skiing.

There's a pier in the village with daily boat service to Hat Rin Beach on Koh Phangan, departing at 9:30 am and 3:30 pm. The fare is 50 baht, and the trip takes about 40 minutes.

There are at this writing, 20 bungalow facilities in Bophut, the most charming of which is **Ziggy Stardust**. Owned and operated by ebullient Ja and her partner Rolf, Ziggy Stardust is an intimate family-run operation tastefully

Bophut Beach has clean white sand and calm water, which makes the bay excellent for water skiing.

designed entirely in the Thai style and features a beautifully manicured tropical garden. Ziggy Stardust (Ja named the place after her favorite David Bowie album) has about a dozen small-to-medium sized bungalows for 300-500 baht, and another dozen large, luxuriously appointed Thai cottages with a/c, modern bathrooms with hot-water, and refrigerators–all for 1,600 baht, including breakfast. There's also a beachside bar, a very good restaurant, and weekly diving and fishing expeditions on a converted Chinese junk out to Koh Tao.

About 100 meters (330 feet) towards the village from Ziggy's, located right on the beach, is a small inn called **The Lodge**, operated by expat Irishman and old Samui hand David Hill and his Thai wife Tim. The Lodge has ten clean, comfortable rooms, all tastefully furnished and facing the sea, for 750 baht/night. David also has a catamaran and large power boat available for rent by the hour or day for diving, fishing, and sailing expeditions to neighboring islands or water skiing in Bophut Bay.

If you're looking for something cheaper, try **Sunny** or **Sala Thai** on the west end of Bophut, where bungalows go for 100-300 baht per night.

There are a few interesting shops in Bophut. Across from The Lodge stands **Tudor House**, which specializes in Lanna silver and textiles from northern Thailand. At the east end of the village is a batik and hand-painted T-shirt shop called **Hand and Mind**, owned by talented Samui artist Phakdee, who designs and produces all his work on the premises. Phakdee creates his original batiks from a blend of Eastern and Western styles, combining both traditional and pop motifs. A custom designed batik or T-shirt made to your specifications takes 3-4 days to produce.

There are about a dozen eateries in Bophut, three of them quite good. At the east end of the village, across from Hand and Mind, is **Tid's**, a family restaurant featuring Thai cuisine and fresh seafood. The grilled shark steak is particularly good. Tid's also offers a selection of ten varieties of potent herbal tonic wines. Made with traditional Thai and Chinese medicinal herbs bearing such revealing names as "Buffalo Power," "Sex Appeal," "Tiger," and "For Old Men Only," they stimulate hormone production and claim to be recommended for amorous couples as well as swinging singles.

About 100 meters (330 feet) up the lane back towards Route 4169, where the road turns left toward Big Buddha, is a small eatery called **Le Bateau**, which prepares an eclectic blend of French, Belgian, and Thai cuisine. Perhaps the best food in Bophut, however, and certainly with the most tasteful dining ambiance, is Ziggy Stardust. This is especially true at night when the daily catch of fresh seafood is displayed on ice at the entrance and cooked to your specifications. Worth special mention is the charcoal grilled fish and prawns, stirfried vegetables, and coconut cream chicken soup (*tom ka gai*).

Songtao taxis plying the main road do not actually enter Bophut Village. They drop you off or pick you up at the turn-off from Route 4169, or, if you're heading to or from Big Buddha, at the corner of Route 4172 near Le Bateau.

It's only a short stroll from there to the village. At night, especially late, there are no taxis available, but for those who wish to boogie late into the night at Chaweng, there is a special private "night-owl" cab that leaves Bophut Village at 10:30 pm which drops you off at the bars and discos in Chaweng, and returns to Bophut around 3:00 am.

Big Buddha Beach To get to Big Buddha Beach from Bophut, head east on Route 4171 towards the airport rather than continuing south on Route 4169, which leads directly to Chaweng.

Big Buddha (*Phra Yai*) takes its name from the 12-meter (40 foot) tall statue of Buddha sitting in tranquil repose on a knoll at the monastery and temple complex of **Koh Fan**, a small islet connected to Samui by a causeway. This statue is one of Samui's foremost sightseeing attractions and will be discussed in detail in the section on temples. (see p. 90)

Like Bophut, Big Buddha is one of Samui's more peaceful beaches, with a smooth and sandy shore line and calm waters. Though it doesn't have its own village, there is an arcade of shops and eateries below the temple grounds on nearby Koh Fan. There's also an interesting selection of traditional Thai handicrafts at a shop called **Fahmui Antiques**, located on Route 4171 near the beach.

Big Buddha Beach currently has about a dozen bungalow facilities, ranging in price from 150 to 1,500 baht. For small, friendly family-run bunga- lows, try **Sunset Song** or **Big Buddha Bungalow**, where cabins go for 150-250 baht. For fancier accommodations with a/c, you might try **Farn Bay Resort** or **Nara Lodge**, for 1,000-1,500/night. The latter has a seaside swimming pool.

A boat makes daily runs across to **Hat Rin** (Rin Beach) on Koh Phangan from a landing pier near the causeway to Koh Fan, departing at 3:30 pm. The fare is 50 baht and the trip takes 40 minutes. Snorkelers will find a colorful coral reef off **Koh Som**, another small offshore islet located about two km (1.25 miles) beyond Koh Fan.

Choeng Mon Beach If you continue on Route 4071 past Big Buddha, the road skirts around the island's northeast headland and provides access to the beaches of Choeng Mon. This remote and quiet corner of the island with several scenic capes and bays that have only recently been developed has no villages, so each resort forms a little world unto itself.

There are about a dozen facilities scattered along the beaches of Choeng Mon between Cape Thongson and Cape Kathong, including one of the most exclusive luxury resorts on the island, the **Imperial Tongsai Bay**. This

Tropical island aficionados claim the hammock to be the most comfortable accommo- dation of all.

58

(preceding page) The private suites of the extravagant Boat House Samui Hotel are renovated wooden rice barges, which are quite nice inside.

beautifully designed property is built into a terraced headland overlooking a quiet cove with its own private beach. It has spacious air-conditioned bungalows, a large swimming pool, tennis courts, and extensive marine recreation facilities, all of which cost its guests 4,500-6,500 baht per night.

On the other cape of the same cove, the Imperial has built the extravagant **Boat House Samui Hotel**, a three-storied U-shaped hotel enclosing a swimming pool and 34 renovated wooden rice barges which have been converted into private suites. Although quite nice inside, the barges seem crowded together and look like a flotilla of galleys run aground. Rates here run from about 3,300 baht for rooms in the hotel wing to 6,000 baht for the "barge" suites.

The 33-bungalow **Sun Sand Resort** is one of the more established facilities at Choeng Mon, with a roped-off ocean pool in the cove below it and bungalows costing 950 baht per night. Right next door to the Boat House you'll find a funky low-budget hostel called **Island View**, favored by hip backpackers. It's quiet, private, and a good bargain with its 15 simple huts going for 50-

The luxurious Imperial Tongsai Bay resort at Choeng Mon Beach has tennis courts and extensive marine recreation facilities

200 baht per night. Within a stone's throw across the beach from Island View sits **Hoh Fan Yai**, an islet that can be reached by foot during low tide.

Yai Noi Bay Between Choeng Mon and Chaweng, is a scenic boulder-strewn cove facing Yai Noi Bay. Your choice of bungalows here is either **I.K.K.** (300-500 baht) or **Coral Bay Resort** (1,500-2,200 baht, including breakfast). The shoreline is rocky, which is not good for swimmers and sun bathers, but the coral reef provides good snorkeling, and it lies within paddling or wading distance of **Koh Matlang**, a small offshore isle which marks the beginning of Samui's famous Chaweng Beach.

Chaweng Beach Chaweng is the Waikiki of Koh Samui: seven kms (4.5 miles) of pearly white sand beach running along a crescent shoreline on the island's east coast. The water is clear and clean, and often the waves break big enough for board and body surfing. You can reach Chaweng by following Route 4171 south from Choeng Mon, or more directly by taking Route 4169 straight down from Bophut.

Chaweng actually consists of three sections: North Chaweng, 1.5 kms (one mile) long, includes the area from Koh Matlang south to "The Island" resort; Hat Chaweng ("Chaweng Beach") from "the Island resort" to Laem Koh Faan, which is 2.5 km (1.5 miles) long, and Chaweng Noi ("Little Chaweng ") which runs from the small headland of beach of Laem Koh Faan to the steep cape at Coral Cove about 3.5 km (2.2 miles). The best beaches, the most bungalows, and all of the night life are located in the central "Hat Chaweng" section.

Although there's a small village on Route 4169 called Ban Chaweng, this is not actually where the "action" is. Central Chaweng Beach has its own strip of shops, restaurants, bars, and discos running parallel to the beach. At the northern end of this strip you'll find the **Black Cat Center**, a Thai style entertainment complex which includes a night club where pretty Thai song-stresses sing a medley of romantic Thai ballads. Here also rests a group of Pattaya style open-air bars catering to a largely male *farang* clientele, with flocks of female cupbearers keeping the beers topped off.

The center section of the strip features a new development called the **Chaweng Arcade**, where you'll find the **Wild Orchid Cafe and Kitchen**, which, by popular acclaim, ranks as one of the best places to eat on the island. Operated by a charming long-term Samui resident named Aew, the Wild Orchid features exotic Thai food, classic cocktails, fancy ice creams, and gourmet coffees, including the best Irish Coffee this side of Bangkok. It has both indoor and outdoor terrace seating, with a separate section upstairs specializing in health foods.

Directly in front of the Wild Orchid is the **Jazz Bar**, managed by Chino, another old Samui hand who hails from Paris. This is one of Chaweng's most popular rendezvous, featuring good drinks, good music, and good "vibes."

CHAWENG BEACH

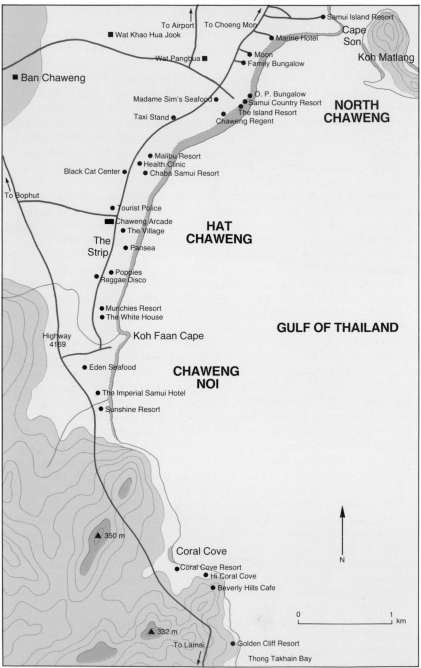

To Airport
To Choeng Mon
■ Wat Khao Hua Jook
● Samui Island Resort
Cape Son
● Marine Hotel
Koh Matlang
Wat Pangbua ■
● Moon
● Family Bungalow
■ Ban Chaweng
● O. P. Bungalow
Madame Sim's Seafood ●
● Samui Country Resort
NORTH CHAWENG
Taxi Stand ●
● The Island Resort
● Chaweng Regent

● Malibu Resort
● Health Clinic
Black Cat Center ●
● Chaba Samui Resort

To Bophut

● Tourist Police
■ Chaweng Arcade
● The Village
The Strip
● Pansea
HAT CHAWENG

● Poppies
● Reggae Disco

● Munchies Resort
● The White House

Highway 4169
Koh Faan Cape

GULF OF THAILAND

● Eden Seafood
CHAWENG NOI

● The Imperial Samui Hotel

● Sunshine Resort

▲ 350 m

N

Coral Cove
● Coral Cove Resort
● Hi Coral Cove
● Beverly Hills Cafe

0   1
km

▲ 332 m

To Lamai
● Golden Cliff Resort
Thong Takhain Bay

Next door to the Wild Orchid is **La Terrasse**, a good place for breakfast and afternoon tea. Just around the corner from here is the **Oriental Gallery**, where you'll find a good selection of silver and silk, antiques, and traditional Thai handicrafts. As of this writing, the rest of the shop-fronts occupying the Chaweng Arcade have not yet been occupied, but already the place is becoming one of Samui's major hot spots.

Nearby you'll also find two of Chaweng's most popular discos—the **Green Mango** and **Reggae**—where one can dance till the crack of dawn. Whoever established the Reggae must be a die-hard Bob Marley fan, for images of his dread locks and wry smile are plastered in every corner, including an interesting collection of Bob Marley T-shirts gleaned from around the world. Other restaurants located along the Central Chaweng strip include **Madame Sims's Seafood**, **Lotus Chinese Restaurant**, the **Pig Sty**, and **Eden**.

There are already 66 bungalow and resort facilities along Chaweng, with more cropping up every month in spite of dwindling space along the beach. On Central Hat Chaweng is a trio of bungalow facilities designed and operated by Oi, an architect and entrepreneur who after many years in Europe decided to return to her native Thailand and settle on Koh Samui. **The White House** is the oldest of the three and very popular with veteran visitors. Its recently renovated bungalows are tucked into a dense tropical garden and rent for about

Famous Chaweng Beach, seven kilometers of pearly white sand with clean, clear water, has the best swimming of Koh Samui, plus the best restaurants and bars.

1,200 baht/night. A few hundred meters north is **The Village**, where cosy cottages cost 1,200-1,800 baht. The Village also has a beautiful garden setting, as well as a good alfresco restaurant facing the sea. Next door is **The Princess Village**, featuring two dozen refurbished old Thai-style houses shipped from the former Thai capital of Ayutthaya. These are elevated all-wood (much of it teak) structures decorated entirely with traditional Thai furniture and fixtures, with modern bathrooms attached, a/c, and a fridge. The houses are set around a landscaped lotus pool and rent for 1,900 baht per night.

Midway between the White House and The Village is **Poppies**, a sister resort of the famous Poppies of Bali and managed by the same group. Located on an excellent strip of beach in Central Chaweng, Poppies is set in a beautifully landscaped garden with ponds, waterfalls, and a swimming pool built among natural rocks. It has a beachfront Thai pavilion restaurant that serves gourmet Thai and Western cuisine which is surrounded by 24 exquisitely appointed Thai style cottages with garden bathrooms, sunken hot-water tubs, verandas, and in-house videos. Poppies also has a catamaran and power boat available for rent by the hour or day for fishing, diving, and sailing excursions to neighboring islands. You'll often find a contingent of the Bali crowd lounging around this exclusive hang-out. The bungalows rent for about 2,500 baht/night.

On the northern end of Central Chaweng is **The Island** resort, which has become a popular outpost for visitors from the Mediterranean island of Ibiza. It has a nice restaurant and bar by the sea and features monthly full-moon parties on the beach and terrace. Its 40 bungalows range from 500-1,500 baht per night.

If you wish to stay close to the "action" in Chaweng but don't want to pay the ritzy rates charged by the prime resorts along the central strip, your best bet is to pick one of the small, modest facilities of North Chaweng or plunk down at the other end of the beach at Chaweng Noi, where one can still find simple rustic bungalows for only 100-300 baht. **Charlie's**, about 100 meters north of the Wild Orchid Cafe along the main strip, is the only budget accommodation on Central Chaweng beach.

Regardless of where you choose to stay on Koh Samui, Central Chaweng still has the best swimming beach and the best restaurants and bars, so you'll probably want to spend some time sporting here. Besides swimming and sun bathing, Chaweng has facilities for wind surfing, snorkeling, scuba diving, parasailing, water skiing, fishing, and sailing. And if that's not enough to keep you amused, you can do some bar hopping at the seaside saloons along the beach, where you're bound to meet some interesting characters.

Coral Cove and Thong Takhain Bay Proceeding due south on Route 4169 for a couple of kilometers the road ascends a steep headland which separates Chaweng from Lamai. Here you'll find scenic cliffside Coral Cove, where there are three hostels tucked into the hillside overlooking Chaweng Bay: **Coral Cove Resort**, **Coral Cove Chalet**, and **Hi Coral Cove**, all of which offer basic bungalows ranging in price from 50 baht (without private bathroom) to 250 baht (with bathroom and fan). Huge boulders line the shore here, and the offshore coral reef provides some of the best snorkeling on the island. At the top of the rise in the road sits the **Beverly Hills Cafe**, which is a good place to stop for a drink and savor some of the most spectacular scenery on the island.

Continuing south towards Lamai, the road dips down and around Thong Takhain Bay, where a sign points seaward to the **Samui Yacht Club**. This is a new up-market resort with 42 comfortable, spacious bungalows, each equipped with a queen-size *and* single bed, a/c, fridge, hot bath, closed-circuit TV, and bedside telephone. It has a private white sand beach (a good place for ladies who like to sun bathe topless), as well as a swimming pool, poolside bar/restaurant, island tour service, and marine recreation facilities. Cabanas here cost 3,300-4,300 baht, making it expensive for long stays but worth it for a few days of pampered privacy, especially if you have more money than time to spend on your holiday.

Aerial view of Coral Cove, where the offshore coral reef provides some of the best snorkeling on Koh Samui.

Lamai Beach One kilometer (.6 mile) beyond Thong Takhain Bay lies Lamai, which, after Chaweng, is Koh Samui's second most popular beach. In general, bungalows run a bit cheaper here than Chaweng, the crowd tends to be a bit younger, and foot-loose, and the scene cleaves closer to funky pop than the chic jet-set tastes of Chaweng.

Ban Lamai itself has several points of interest, including the **Lamai Cultural Hall** (see "Inland and Upland" chapter for details), a few good Western bakeries, some shops and snack bars, and a scuba center, but the main focus of activity in Lamai is down along the strip near the beach.

This strip looks a lot like one of those slapdash cowboy boom towns in the Old American West, a sort of "Lamai Gulch," with saloons and shops, restaurants and cafes, lined cheek-to-jowl along its pot-holed dirt lanes. By day you can engage in all sorts of water sports along central Lamai's extensive beach, pump iron with local body builders at the **Lamai Gym**, or sign up for Thai boxing (*Muay Thai*) lessons at the **Flamingo Gym**, which also stages matches open to *farang* challengers.

But the real action in Lamai Gulch starts after dark. There are plenty of restaurants here, among which you'll find good European food at **Papa's**, Italian fare and espresso coffee at **Ciao Pinko**, seafood and Thai food at **Flamingo**, and good home-style Thai dishes at **Thai Cat**, located across from the Mix Pub.

After dinner, you might want to hit some of the saloons located along the narrow side lanes of the Gulch. Most of them employ bevies of barmaids to chat up unaccompanied men while others offer nightly feature films on video.

At the **Flamingo Party House** you'll find Lamai's most popular disco. It doesn't start swinging till midnight, when suddenly gaggles of giggling girls appear on the scene to preen and strut their stuff. But predators beware: appearances can be very deceiving in the strobe streaked shadows of Thai discos, so it's easy to mistake the true gender of your intended prey.

About 100 meters (330 feet) north of the Flamingo is another big bar and disco called **Mix Pub**, which has a disc jockey, good sound system and sometimes a live band as well. There's also a spacious open terrace where you can drink and chat without being deafened by the high-decibel music inside.

Central Lamai Beach has a choice of at least 40 different types of bungalow facilities, ranging in price from 50 to 2,000 baht, with most in the 300-600 baht range. If it's not the peak tourist season, you can usually negotiate good discounts at these mid-priced hostels, especially if you're staying for a few weeks or more. At the northern end is one of the nicest accommodations in Lamai, the **Pavilion**, which has a good beach, a swimming pool, a seaside restaurant, and 25 a/c wood-and-bamboo bungalows which include a fridge and mini-bar for 1,800 baht/night. An additional 16 rooms in a side wing rent for 1,200 baht.

LAMAI BEACH

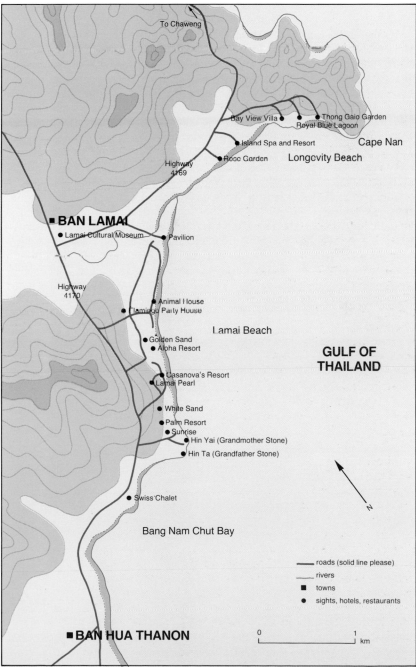

To Chaweng

Bay View Villa ● ● ● Thong Gaio Garden
Royal Blue Lagoon

● Island Spa and Resort
Cape Nan

Highway 4169
● Rose Garden   Longevity Beach

■ **BAN LAMAI**
● Lamai Cultural Museum   ● Pavilion

Highway 4170
● Animal House
● Flamingo Party House

Lamai Beach

● Golden Sand
● Aloha Resort

GULF OF THAILAND

● Casanova's Resort
● Lamai Pearl

● White Sand
● Palm Resort
● Sunrise
● Hin Yai (Grandmother Stone)
● Hin Ta (Grandfather Stone)

N

● Swiss Chalet

Bang Nam Chut Bay

─── roads (solid line please)
─── rivers
■ towns
● sights, hotels, restaurants

■ **BAN HUA THANON**

0   1
└─────────────────┘ km

Further down the beach, **Aloha Resort** has a good reputation and a good restaurant. Its 37 bungalows range in price from 350 to 1,700 baht. A few hundred meters beyond Aloha is **Casanova's Resort**, with 20 cosy cabins built into a landscaped hillside shaded by a coconut grove. With a pool and sun deck, rooms rent for 1,000-2,000 baht/night. Budget-minded travelers might move further down to the lower end of Central Lamai and check out **White Sand**, **Palm**, and **Sunrise**, where one can still find bargain bungalows for 50-250 baht.

Past the headland where the famous Grandpa and Grandma Rocks stare stonily out to sea is a shallow coral reef cove facing onto **Bang Nam Chut Bay**. Most of the year the water here is too shallow for swimming, but during the latter part of the rainy season (September-December), when seas are too rough elsewhere around the island, Lower Lamai offers some of the best swimming on the island. On a promontory overlooking the bay rests the **Swiss Chalet**, a quiet, well-established retreat with only seven uncrowded bungalows that rent for 450 baht/night, plus six seaview rooms in a new wing on the beach, at 900 baht. The restaurant here prepares Swiss as well as Thai cuisine at reasonable prices. Below the Swiss Chalet are a few more bungalows with rock bottom prices and simple no-frills facilities.

Koh Samui is noted for its shore to shore coconut palms and an abundance of seaside bungalows. The combination make it the proverbial tropical paradise.

Na Kai Bay and Cape Set Lower Lamai ends at **Ban Hua Thanon,** an old Muslim fishing village that looks out on to Na Kai Bay. There's a colorful open-air fish and produce market at the lower end of the village, with a fleet of weathered old fishing boats moored in the bay's shallows.

In Hua Thanon, Route 4169 makes a sharp right turn and continues inland through coconut plantations for 15 km (10 miles) directly across the island to the west coast and back up to Nathon. About 200 meters (660 feet) after this turn in the village, there's a left turn which takes you onto Route 4170, a road that skirts around the southern and southwestern shores of Samui before reconnecting with 4169 halfway up the west coast. 4170 provides access to the capes and bays along the southern coast.

Na Kai Bay has a rocky shoreline and shallow reef which allow for good snorkeling if not good swimming. One km after the turn-off from 4169, there's a dirt road heading seaward that takes you to the **Cosy Resort** and **Hilton Garden**. The Cosy has nine simple bungalows that rent for 200 baht, while Hilton Garden, which has a large pool, offers 40 a/c bungalows at 800-1,000 baht.

A further half km down 4170 there's another left turn onto a dirt road which leads to three remote and tranquil hostels. The first is Samui Orchid Resort, with 64 rooms ranging in price from 650-1,200 baht. Further down the coast lies **Nathien**, with eight nicely arranged bungalows for 650 baht. Follow the winding dirt road all the way to the tip of Cape Set and you'll reach a pleasant, very private accommodation called **Laem Set Inn**. Bungalows here used to go for under 500 baht, but after being reviewed in a few trendy American travel magazines prices shot up to 650-2,500 baht. Nevertheless, it's a very nice place to stay if you're looking for complete peace and solitude. English proprietor W. D. Parry has a knack for making his guests feel very much at home and his restaurant serves good food, which is fortunate since it's a long walk to the nearest next place to eat. There's also a small pool by the beach.

Bang Kao Bay Continuing west on Route 4170, the road follows the southern coast along Bang Kao Bay, but you have to take one of the various dirt roads for about one km (.6 mile) seaward to reach the shore.

Bang Kao Bay covers the five km (3 miles) of coast line between Cape Set and Cape Sor, and like Na Kai Bay, the beach is quite rocky with an extensive coral reef offshore that's good for snorkeling and fishing. There are a few simple bungalow facilities along this bay, such as **Diamond Villa** and **River Garden**, where huts go for 100-200 baht. Near the tip of Cape Sor you'll find a couple of old *chedis* (stupas), which are worth a visit for those interested in temple archaeology.

Thong Krut Bay Next stop past Cape Sor is a tiny village called Ban Thong Krut, which faces onto Thong Krut Bay on the southwest corner of the island. Here you'll find a solitary hostel called **Thong Krut**, with seven no-frills huts for 100-200 baht.

If you'd like to visit the nearby island of **Koh Taen** (also known as "Island of No Dog"). there is unscheduled boat service available from Ban Thong Krut. The boat men charge a minimum of 100 baht for the three km (2 mile) crossing, regardless of how many people are aboard. There's a small 10 bungalow facility there called **Koh Taen Resort**, where rates run 100-150 baht, in case you wish to spend a few days exploring this island.

Phangka Bay Two km (1.25 mile) past Ban Thong Krut, Route 4170 makes a sharp hairpin turn to the right and proceeds due north up the west coast. At this point is a left turn onto a dirt road which winds 2.5 km (1.6 miles) down to Phangka Bay, also known as Emerald Cove.

This is probably the most secluded cove on the island, so if it's absolute isolation you're seeking, this might be the place for you. There are three facilities located here—**Sea Gull**, **Pearl**, and **Emerald Cove**—with huts costing 100-150 baht. The sunset views are quite spectacular here, and you can spend many leisurely hours strolling through the coconut groves and exploring scenic Cape Hin Khom, which cradles the southern end of Emerald Cove. Be informed, however, that during low tide the beach becomes a mud flat and is not conducive to swimming or other water sports. This is a cove for landlubbers and recluses, not surfers and beach lovers.

Thong Yang Bay The next bay with resort facilities is Thong Yang Bay, located midway up the west coast, between Phangka Bay and Nathon. This is where the vehicle ferry from Don Sak pier on the mainland arrives. To get there from Phangka Bay, return to Route 4170 and proceed north six km (4 miles), where the road reconnects with 4169, then continue north another two km (1.25 mile) and turn left onto Route 4174, which leads out toward the ferry pier.

Thong Krut Bay, on the west coast of Koh Samui, has exquisite sunsets.

There are several bungalow facilities on Thong Yang Bay, the best of which is the **Coco Cabana**, located in a quiet cove about half a km south of the ferry pier. It has a nice strip of beach along calm waters and 20 cosy bungalows that rent for 150-250 baht. This is a good place to stay if you want to keep away from crowds, avoid night life, and keep your expenses down.

Chon Khram Bay A mushroom-shaped, coral reefed cape separates Thong Yang Bay from Chon Khram Bay. which is a big and broad bay with good beaches, placid waters, and sweeping sunset views across the sea. Route 4174 skirts along its shoreline en route to the Don Sak ferry pier.

The place to stay here is **Lipa Lodge**, where bungalows go for 200-450 baht. It has a decent bar and restaurant with reasonable prices, and it's quiet. It's also only five km (3 miles) from Nathon, in the event you wish to stay near town. For somewhat fancier accommodations with a/c, you might try the **Plern Resort** next door, where bungalows run 600-1,200 baht.

Back to Nathon From the junction at Route 4174, 4169 continues north another five km (3 miles) back to Nathon, completing its 50-km (31-mile) circuit around the island. 50 km doesn't seem like much distance by Western freeway standards, but on Koh Samui the variety of different beaches and coves to which it gives access makes it seem more like 500 km. All visitors to Samui should make the round-the-island trip at least once, preferably by rented car or motorbike, just to experience the extraordinary diversity the island offers.

Tropical Bungalows

The word "bungalow" comes from the Hindi term *bangla*, which literally means "house or cottage in the Bengal style." Webster's Dictionary defines bungalow as "a lightly built, low sweeping single-story house or cottage of the Far East that is usually thatched or tiled and surrounded by a veranda." Westerners accustomed to dwellings built of stone, brick, and concrete will find a delightfully different ambiance in the tropical bungalow, which is specifically designed and constructed to suit the climate and other environmental conditions of the tropics.

Wood, thatch, and bamboo are the primary materials in a tropical bungalow: anything bulkier would feel oppressively hot and heavy in the humid heat of the tropics. Roofs are steeply peaked to permit hot air to rise and dissipate inside and rain to run off quickly outside. Beams are usually left exposed and ceiling panels omitted for maximum ventilation. "Low-sweeping" refers to the sweeping eaves which extend up to three feet beyond the walls all around the bungalow, shading the perpetually open windows from the sun and protecting them from the rain. Windows are usually large and unglassed to permit constant circulation of fresh air, but screened to keep out mosquitoes and flies.

Most tropical bungalows consist of one large room that functions as both parlor and bedroom plus a bathroom. Wall partitions reduce circulation of air increasing the heat and are therefore usually omitted. The traditional tropical bath, particularly in Thailand, is performed by using a bowl to ladle cold water over one's body from a large ceramic holding vat that's always kept full. Though many Thais as well as *farangs* still prefer this traditional method, called *ap-nam* ("pouring water"), bungalows today are often equipped with modern Western bathrooms, complete with showers, tubs, sinks, and toilets. On the other hand, old-fashioned tropical bungalows, such as those on Koh Phangan and Koh Tao, have no private bathroom at all on the premises. Instead, there are separate communal bathhouses and outhouses located outside.

Verandas are a major hallmark of the tropical bungalow, and often the most important part of the house. While some bungalows have verandas extending around the entire perimeter of the house, most have a large covered porch only in front. This functions as an additional room and is the place where people spend most of their time at home.

You'll also notice that most tropical bungalows are built well off the ground on stilts, with stairs leading up to the edge of the veranda,

not directly to the door. This keeps the house from flooding during heavy monsoon rains and permits circulation of cooling air beneath the house during the hot dry season. It also discourages snakes and other creepy crawling creatures from entering the house.

Traditional Thai houses rank among the most artful expressions of tropical bungalow architecture, and Koh Samui excels in the design and construction of the beach variety of this form of housing. You'll find a wide range of styles among Samui's bungalows, from simple thatched A-frames with no bathrooms to full-blown Thai villas elegantly furnished and equipped with modern bathrooms and air-conditioning.

Good examples of the differences as well as common denominators between the basic and the deluxe style of Thai bungalow are the accommodations at Ziggy Stardust in Bophut. On one side of the garden stands a row of typical no-frills beach bungalows, made of thatch, bamboo slats, and matting. Across the garden is a row of deluxe Thai cottages made with a variety of polished hardwoods, equipped with modern hot-water baths and air-conditioning. Furnished with elaborately carved hardwood furniture, they are fronted by spacious verandas. You'll also find good examples at Sea Fan on Maenam and the Pavilion on Lamai.

At the Princess Village in Chaweng, all bungalows are full-fledged traditional Thai houses transported to Samui from the ancient capital of Ayutthaya. Veritable architectural antiques constructed largely of teak wood, these charming old dwellings have been refurbished with modern plumbing and electricity to provide contemporary comforts, but the original ambiance has been well preserved with traditional Thai fixtures and furnishings. These are more than beach bungalows: they're classic Thai houses with all the trimmings.

Though wood, thatch, and bamboo are the traditional construction materials, many proprietors these days are also incorporating stone, brick, and glass in their bungalows, especially to allow for air-conditioning, which requires good insulation. Still, even such modern versions rely on traditional materials for furniture, trim, and architectural accents. The elegant cottages at Poppies on Chaweng are good examples of this blended style.

True connoisseurs of tropical islands always opt to stay in cosy, free-standing bungalows rather than regimented rooms in winged, multi-storied hotels, for the tropical bungalow is as much a part of the landscape as the coconut palms.

Inland and Upland Attractions

Hin Lat Waterfall About 2 km (1.25 miles) south of Nathon on Route 4169, a few hundred meters past the bus station, you'll come to the intersection of Route 4172. Turn left towards the mountains and one km up the road you'll come to the river which leads up to Hin Lat Waterfall. To get to the waterfall itself requires a further 1.5 km (1 mile) hike upstream along the boulder strewn river bed. It's a scenic, pleasant walk and well worth the 30-40 minute effort. Along the way, the river forms a variety of small pools and rivulets where one can stop to wallow like a water buffalo or simply dangle your feet to cool off. It's a good idea to bring along a bottle of water and some fresh fruit to refresh yourself as you hike.

Across the river from the parking lot and snack stalls is a tranquil Buddhist meditation retreat called **Suan Dhamapala**, a traditional Thai forest monastic retreat surrounded by lush tropical vegetation and serenaded by the symphonic sounds of birds, cicadas, and the gentle splash of the river. If you wish to wander around this Buddhist garden and visit the shrine hall, be sure that you're properly attired.

Na Muang Waterfall 11 km (7 miles) south of Nathon on Route 4169 is the turn-off to "Na Muang Waterfall," located about one km up the side road. There's a good Thai restaurant called **Phaluang** set in a Thai style house located on the corner of the turn-off, in case you decide to stop for a bite to eat.

Na Muang Waterfall cascades in a rippling sheet 40 meters (132 feet) down a sheer slab of stone, forming a pool at the bottom in which you may wade and splash around (best to see during the rainy season when it can be quite dramatic). The waterfall is only a few steps from the parking lot, and it's surrounded by a densely wooded grotto which, if it's not too crowded or littered when you visit, affords some nice spots for a picnic. Unfortunately crowds of raucous Thai picnickers who often arrive by the pick-up truck load can sometimes detract from the natural serenity of the spot. Avoid visiting mid-days or weekends if you can.

Overlap Stone In Lower Lamai there's a sign marked "Overlap Stone" pointing inland along a narrow dirt road. You'll need a four-wheel drive jeep to get all the way up there on wheels, otherwise just drive your car or motorbike about halfway up and walk the rest of the way. If you don't have a vehicle of you own, have a *songtao* drop you off at the entrance and hike up the trail on foot. It's only a one-km (.6–mile) walk, albeit very steep at the upper end.

The Overlap Stone is a tall boulder perched precariously on a promontory overlooking Lamai Beach. You'll find a landscaped refreshment stall and small six-hut bungalow facility here, owned and operated by a hospitable, warm-hearted man named Bancha. He rents his rustic huts out for about 100 baht

(less if it's off season), and if it's complete seclusion conducive for meditating you're looking for, this is the place. A couple of small palm leaf gazebos offer beautiful panoramic views of the beaches and coral reefs along the southeastern shores of Samui. You'll find lots of cashew trees along the trail and endless acres of coconut plantation. If you have enough energy to spare, an additional two km (1.25 mile) hike straight up the trail beyond Overlap Stone brings you right up to the top of one of Samui's peaks. It's a great trek and gives you a vivid impression of the island's interior terrain and highland flora, which constitute an entirely different ambiance from the beaches.

Samui Hin Samui Hin is one of the highest points on Koh Samui (573 m– 1890 feet) and the source of the river which feeds Na Muang Waterfall. There are several ways to get there. If you continue along the trail beyond Overlap Stone for approximate 6-7 km (4 miles) to the very end, it eventually reaches Samui Hin. There's another trail marked "Samui Hin," that cuts inland off Route 4169 about 2.5 km (1.6 miles) west of Ban Hua Thanon, across the road from Wat Khumaram. From there it's a steep four km (2.5 miles) climb to the top. There's also an 11 km (6.9 mile) trail that starts near the Lamai Cultural Hall in Ban Lamai, but this is only for hardy mountaineers, and it's best to take

along a guide. On all upland hikes, be sure to wear appropriate shoes and long pants to protect against bugs and brambles, and, of course, a sufficient supply of drinking water.

Grandfather Stone and Grandmother Stone (Hin Ta, Hin Yai) These two graphically genital geological formations are probably the most frequently photographed sights on Samui. They're located at the tip of the headland which separates Central Lamai from Lower Lamai, at the end of a dirt lane off Route 4169, clearly marked by a sign, "Hin Ta, Hin Yai."

Grandfather Stone (Hin Ta) bulges proudly toward the sky from an elevated perch on a pile of boulders at the cusp of the cape, while Grandmother Stone (Hin Yai) lies splayed in a surf-washed cleft about 40 meters (130 feet) nearby. Both face due east towards the rising sun.

The ancient Chinese science of geomancy (*feng-shui*, literally "wind and water") explains morphological/geophysical formations such as these as the result of aeons of molding by the forces of wind and water in conjunction with the intentional direction of indigenous terrestrial spirits who wish to take elemental form. In the case of Hin Ta and Hin Yai, the spirits at work are obviously fertility spirits, and many Asian visitors, especially from Taiwan and Japan, approach them as highly auspicious totems. Even more remarkable is the obvious fact that Grandmother has been formed primarily by water (a *Yin* or female force), while Grandfather has been shaped mainly by wind (a *Yang* or male force). Fact or fancy, even if you don't believe in geomancy, these vividly

Sturdy macaque monkeys are trained to scurry up the coconut trees to harvest the ripe nuts.

suggestive formations will probably make you pause to speculate about the preternatural forces at work here.

Coral Buddha Stones About one km east of Ban Hua Thanon on Route 4169 you'll see a sign pointing inland to the "Coral Buddhas," located about 100 meters (330 feet) up a narrow dirt trail. In a clump of tall grass on the left side of the trail sit two large Buddha statues of uncertain origin carved in coral stone. The base of one has crumbled, leaving the head tilted askew, but the other image remains in meditative repose. These images are still revered by local Buddhists, who occasionally leave votive offerings here, but they're probably of interest only to travelers with a taste for Buddhist statuary.

Coconut Monkeys Among Koh Samui's most hard working residents are the crews of sturdy macaque monkeys trained to scurry up coconut trees and harvest ripe nuts. You can catch their act at the **Med Sai** bungalow, located about three km (1.8 miles) north of Nathon on Route 4169, where for 50 baht per person a handler will put his simian harvester through its paces for you.

Trained to harvest only the ripe nuts, as soon as they've picked one tree clean, they leap across to the top of the next tree instead of wasting time and energy coming down and going back up again. A well trained monkey is capable of picking up to 1,000 coconuts per day, and without them Koh Samui's monthly harvest of two million coconuts would never be completed. Macaques are used widely for this purpose in all of southern Thailand, Malaysia, Southern India and Sri Lanka.

Coconut Culture

A tropical island would not be a tropical island without the ubiquitous presence of the tall slender coconut palm waving its long fronds gently in the breeze. For centuries the coconut palm (*Cocos Nucifera*) has been the quintessential symbol of tropical islands all over the world, and virtually every island travel brochure features the palm as a logo. Known throughout the South Pacific as the "Tree of Life," the coconut palm comes in 30 distinct varieties, enjoys an average life span of 60 years, and produces about 75 nuts per year.

If coconuts are the distinguishing feature of tropical islands, then Koh Samui must be one of the coconut capitals of the world. Blanketed from shore to shore and beach to mountain peak with coconut palms, Koh Samui is Thailand's major producer, shipping over two million nuts per month to Bangkok. At 75 nuts per palm per year, you can well imagine how many trees it takes to produce an average monthly crop of two million coconuts! In Koh Samui, coconuts are not just another pretty part of the tropical scenery: they form the backbone of the island's economy and exert a major influence on every aspect of the island's culture.

How does Samui harvest two million coconuts per month? First of all, they wear crash helmets! A number of people are killed each year by falling coconuts in Samui, and while the image of someone getting bonked on the noggin by a falling coconut seems funny, the actual effects are deadly. Secondly, coconut planters in Samui rely on legions of well trained monkeys to scamper up the palms and toss down the ripe nuts. Leaping from palm to palm, a good monkey can pick up to 1,000 nuts per day, which is a lot more than any human could do.

Within Samui, the primary use for coconuts (*ma-prao*) is culinary, and they appear in various forms in all sorts of tasty Thai dishes. The meat of the ripe coconut is scraped from the shell, soaked in hot water, and squeezed to extract a rich buttery essence called "coconut cream," which plays much the same role in Thai cuisine as dairy cream does in Western cooking. Coconut cream is an indispensable ingredient in all curry sauces. The problem with so many curries cooked in Western kitchens is that the cook neglects to add coconut cream, which blends and balances all the various spices and lends its smooth texture and rich nutty flavor to the sauce. Coconut cream is also a primary ingredient in many Thai soups, such as the incomparable Coconut Cream Chicken Soup (*Tom Ka Gai*)

Coconut cream is also the basis of many Thai sweets (*kanom*). All sorts of creamy custards and puddings owe their rich flavor and smooth texture to this versatile condiment, and some of these confections are further enhanced with a generous lacing of freshly grated coconut meat. Fresh Mango with Sticky Rice (*Kao-nee-o Mahmun*), which many connoisseurs regard as the king of Thai desserts, is soaked in thick coconut cream, as are desserts made with bananas, water chestnuts, beans, jellies, and tapioca. One of the tastiest treats of all is fresh coconut ice cream, which is featured on almost every menu in Koh Samui.

Coconut cream also makes delicious drinks, such as the frothy white Pina Colada and cooling Coconut Shake. You can even add coconut cream to coffee instead of using milk. Note that coconut cream, which is extracted from the ripe flesh, is an entirely different product than coconut water, which is the clear fluid found inside tender young green coconuts. Coconut water is a very refreshing beverage in itself, has virtually no calories, and is highly regarded throughout the tropics as an effective coolant to the blood and internal organs. It's a good remedy for hangovers, indigestion, and heart burn.

The coconut palm also yields an alcoholic beverage called *todi*, otherwise known as "poor man's wine" since it costs nothing but the effort of shinnying up the tree to tap the unopened buds of the inflorescence on top. An incision is cut into the bud at night and a small bucket is hung beside it to catch the fluid. Next morning the bucket is retrieved brim full of sweet rich *todi*. It ferments slightly during the night, producing a light alcohol content which grows steadily stronger towards noon, after which it turns sour. It's best to drink it early in the morning.

Todi can also be boiled down to make palm sugar, which can then be fermented to produce palm wine, which in turn may then be distilled to yield a highly potent palm spirit called *arrack*. *Arrack* is the fire water of the tropics. Strangely, however, Samui does not produce *todi*, palm wine, or *arrack*—at least not commercially—though for a price you could probably persuade a planter to tap some *todi* for you. The reason they no longer make these various palm libations in Samui is probably because it's too much trouble and they're no longer poor. It's a lot easier to go to the nearest shop and buy a bottle of beer or whisky.

Besides the nut, coconut palms also produce several other edible delicacies. When the tree blossoms, the inflorescence yields a firm translucent fruit called *luk-dan*, a seasonal treat available only when the trees flower. The naturally sweet nectar extracted from this exotic palm fruit is available year round throughout Thailand in cans and bottles, and anyone with a sweet tooth will be delighted by its luscious taste and syrupy texture. You'll find it canned in the chilled beverage section of most supermarkets and many snack stalls under the "Seaside Coconut Nectar" label.

Anyone who's lived in the tropics for a long time has no doubt observed the excitement aroused by the felling of a coconut palm. Palms have hearts, and when they die, people rush over to extract the grandest gourmet treat the tree has to offer—the peerless Heart of Palm. For each heart of palm that ends up in the kitchen a tree must die, so it's a rather rare delicacy, but if by chance you find it, by all means try it. It has a delicate nutty flavor and a crisp texture similar to fresh bamboo shoots. In Samui, it's either sliced and stir-fried with chili and garlic, or served in soups.

The primary commercial use for coconuts is to produce copra, from which coconut oil is extracted for cooking and canning, soaps and cosmetics. Coconut oil is a great moisturizer for skin and hair parched dry by strong tropical sunlight, and you will find it for sale all over Samui for 10 baht per 100 ml bottle. Unfortunately, processed coconut oil is high in denatured cholesterol and should be avoided in food, although this is not true of coconut cream, water, flesh, inflorescence, nectar, heart, and other freshly extracted edibles. In recent years, methods have been developed to convert coconut oil into diesel fuel, which is about 15 per cent more efficient than petroleum diesel and more environment friendly.

The rest of the tree is also put to practical use. The timber from the trunks of old mature trees is used to build houses, bridges, fences, and furniture. The dried leafy fronds are knotted and woven together to make thatch roofs, walls, and screens. The hairy husks encasing ripe coconuts are used as planters for orchids, stuffing for pillows and mattresses, and ropes, while the hard dried shells are polished and crafted into a variety of attractive household utensils and jewelry items, such as bowls, ladles, cups, spatulas, ear-rings, bracelets, pendants, necklaces, and hair ornaments. These items make great gifts and are available in handicraft and souvenir shops all over the island.

Even the Bible extols the virtues of the palm: in Psalm 92: 12 we read, "The righteous shall flourish like the palm tree." And for Christians, Palm Sunday marks the beginning of the Holy Week which precedes Easter Sunday.

Moreover, the coconut is about the same size and shape as the human head, complete with hair, a hard "skull," and a soft, white, watery interior. Truly, food for thought!

Temples

As one old-timer on Koh Samui wryly notes, "There are lots of beautiful temples in Samui but not very many monks." Unlike the rest of Thailand, where most Buddhist temples and monasteries are well populated with resident monks and novices, the temples of Koh Samui are rather sparsely occupied, lending them an even more tranquil ambiance than elsewhere. Perhaps the paucity of monks is due in part to the island's hedonistic character, and partly due to Koh Samui's distance from mainstream Thailand. Nevertheless, there are a few monks living in most of the monasteries and temples around the island, and they are consistently friendly and helpful to visitors, who in turn should observe proper etiquette in dress and behavior when visiting these spiritual sanctuaries.

Those who wish to gain deeper insights on Buddhism might consider a visit to the **Suanmoke International Buddhist Center**, located across the water on the mainland, about 50 km (31 miles) from Surat Thani on Highway 41, near Chaiya district. Founded by the venerable Thai Buddhist master Buddhadasa Bhikkhu, Suanmoke is an international institute where spiritual seekers from all countries and all walks of life are welcome to come to study and practice the Buddhist teachings under the guidance of experienced English-speaking monks. Suanmoke offers regular ten-day courses of study and meditation in both Thai and English for a tuition/donation of 600 baht, and there are dormitories available for those who wish to stay and study amidst the center's tranquil natural environment.

Big Buddha Temple (Wat Phra Yai) Almost all visitors to Samui sooner or later pay respects to the Big Buddha who sits serenely on a hilltop shrine at the temple on Koh Fan adjacent to Big Buddha Beach. This 12-meter (40 foot) statue has become one of Samui's major landmarks and makes a beautiful photograph silhouetted against the sky at sunset. At the entrance to the temple sits a statue of the smiling, big-bellied *Maitreya*, the "Happy Buddha" who according to Buddhist tradition will be the next Buddha to manifest himself on earth. Inside the courtyard is a shrine dedicated to the Reclining Buddha, a popular motif in Thailand.

Two seven-headed *nagas* (sea dragons) undulate down the staircase that leads up to the Big Buddha on top. There he sits gazing beatifically over Koh Samui, his hands held in the "Touching the Earth" (*Bhumisparsa Mudra*: "Calling the Earth to Witness") gesture which the Buddha is said to have adopted at the moment of his enlightenment. Below is a shrine for making offerings. The colonnade around the base of the statue provides panoramic views of Koh Samui's northern shore line, Koh Phangan, and the nearby offshore islet of Koh Som.

This is also a monastic meditation retreat, and along the shore below the

92

*According to Buddhist tradition, the big-bellied "Happy Buddha" of the
temple of Koh Fan will be the next Buddha to manifest himself on earth.*

statue you'll see a string of tiny one-room *kuti* (meditation huts), built up on
stilts. These are where resident and visiting monks sleep and practice meditation. Down near the parking lot, outside the temple walls, you'll find an arcade
of souvenir and snack shops. Some of the shops carry interesting handicrafts
and hand-made jewelry, but prices tend to be inflated due to the many large
tour groups that come here, so bargain before you buy.

Wat Khunaram 2.5 km (1.6 miles) west of Ban Hua Thanon on the
seaward side of Route 4169 is the arched entry to Wat Khunaram. Located in a
palm shaded compound, this old monastery contains some traditional wooden
buildings which pre-date the age of concrete and steel architecture. Around the
edge of the compound are over a dozen stone *chedis* (stupas), which hold the
remains of deceased abbots and monks. Near the inner entrance stands a sacred
tree with two shrines at the base, and off to the right is a simple shrine hall
housing the intact, mummified remains of the monk Loung Pordeang, a highly
accomplished meditator who died over 20 years ago.

His body sits in the same meditative posture he adopted the day he died,
somewhat shrunken from dehydration, but without any signs of decay.
Throughout Asia this is a universally acknowledged result of having been a
master meditator, and in Thailand the remains of such venerable monks are

Classical Thai temple architecture.

usually preserved in shrines rather than cremated. If a temple has sufficient funds, such remains are often encased in pure gold, but not in this case. Visitors are welcome to make merit by offering incense and garlands at the small altar in front of the glass case in which this remarkable relic sits. This is a sight well worth seeing, especially for modern-minded sceptics who doubt the transformational powers of meditation.

Wat Sumret In the same neighborhood on Route 4169, about one km east of Ban Hua Nathon, directly opposite the trail to the Coral Buddha images, is a dirt road leading a kilometer seaward to Wat Sumret. Here too you will find some beautiful old weathered wooden buildings constructed in the traditional Thai style. There is also a new shrine hall recently built to house the temple's sacred images. The entire complex is nestled in the shade of huge old trees, one of which has a trunk with an eight-foot girth that is claimed to be at least 600 years old. In addition, this temple has an ornate crematorium with a tall fluted chimney off to one side, as well as a few rows of stone *chedis* containing the remains of deceased monks.

Wat Taling Ngam To get to this temple, drive or take a taxi 6.5 km (4 miles) south of Nathon along Route 4169, then turn right onto Route 4170. Continue south about three km (1.8 miles) on 4170 until you come to a huge gate flanked by two life-size stone elephants. This is the entrance to Taling Ngam

Wat Taling Ngam

Village, on the other end of which you'll find the entrance to Wat Taling Ngam.

This is an old temple complex shaded by several ancient banyan trees and a coconut grove. Its claim to fame are the mummified remains of a monk, still undecayed, who died while sitting in meditative equipoise in 1967, similar to that found at Wat Khunaram. An elevated shrine houses his body, the face clearly recognizable, in a glass case placed behind a statue of him. Regardless of whether or not you're a Buddhist, this is certainly a phenomenon worth seeing with your own eyes.

Wat Laem Sor and Khao Chedi At the southern tip of the island, out on Cape Sor (Laem Sor) you'll find "Wat Laem Sor," which is renowned primarily for the old, elegantly constructed

One of two carved coral stone Buddha statues that rest by a trail near Ban Hua Thanon.

chedi named Khao Chedi located in its compound. Nearby stands another ancient *chedi*, which would be of interest to amateur archaeologists as well as Buddhists. To get there take any one of the three dirt roads that leads down to Bang Kao Bay and Cape Sor off Route 4170.

Lamai Cultural Hall At the 90-degree turn on Route 4169 as it passes through Ban Lamai stands the arched entrance to the Lamai Cultural Hall. In an old wooden building there is a cultural museum displaying a variety of ceramics, tools, utensils, hunting gear, musical instruments, and other local artifacts. There's also a temple located in this compound, with several shrines, chedis, and a dozen resident monks who maintain the grounds.

Other Islands

Koh Phangan

If you find Koh Samui too developed or expensive for your taste and budget, perhaps Koh Phangan is the place for you. Even if you're staying on Samui, a few side-trips out to Phangan are well worthwhile.

It is said in Samui that although Koh Phangan is only 14 km (9 miles) away, it's 15 years behind in development. This is welcome news to beach purists who shun crowds and fancy resorts and prefer candlelight to electricity. This situation, however, may not last much longer as developers on Soumi cast their eyes across the water to the virgin shores of bucolic Koh Phangan. Still, for the time being, Koh Phangan remains a convenient escape from the excesses of Samui.

At 190 sq. km (28 sq. miles), Phangan is the largest of Samui's neighboring islets, with a population of about 8,000, most of whom live in the main town and port of Thong Sala. There are currently 124 bungalow facilities scattered along the island's shores, with a total of some 2,100 rooms. Almost all of them are simple thatch and bamboo huts, many without electricity or private baths. Prices range from 30 to 300 baht per night, thus averaging about 70% less than Samui.

Koh Phangan has much the same feeling and style as Phuket did during the 1970s, and indeed many aging hippies have migrated here as places like Goa, Bali, and Phuket have become over-developed. With them came many venerable institutions which old-timers from those heady days will readily recognize: full-moon parties on the beach; open-air yoga classes; home-made bread and yogurt stalls; a flea market; and plenty of rock-and-roll. This scene is not for everyone, but even jet-setters who prefer the comforts and conveniences of Samui's deluxe resorts often like to make day (and night) trips across to Phangan to kick up their heels and swing with the laid-back Bohemians of the backwaters of Koh Phangan.

Getting There

Koh Phangan lies approx. 16 km (10 miles) north of Koh Samui.

By Boat Songserm Travel operates express boats from Nathon Pier in Samui out to Thong Sala on Koh Phangan daily at 10:00 am and 3:00 pm November through May, 10:00 am and 3:30 pm June through October. The fare is 55 baht, and the trip takes 50 minutes. Return trips depart Thong Sala daily at 6:15 am and 11:00 am November through May, 6:15 am and 12:30 pm June through October.

There's also a daily boat from the Bophut Pier in northern Samui to Hat Rin Beach on Phangan at 9:30 am and 3:30 pm, with return runs at 9:00 am and 2:30 pm. The one-way fare is 50 baht, and the trip takes 45 minutes. In addition, there's a daily boat from Big Buddha Beach to Hat Rin at 3:30 pm, with return service at 9:30 am (50 baht, 45 minutes), and from Maenam Beach to Thong Nai Pan Bay in northeast Phangan daily at 11:00 am January through September only, returning at 8:00 am, for 100 baht.

Bear in mind that all boat services to and from Koh Phangan are subject to weather conditions and may therefore be canceled or delayed at the last minute, but generally the schedules are quite reliable, especially during the January through May peak season.

You can reach Koh Phangan directly from Surat Thani's Ban Don Pier via the night ferry, which departs daily at 11:00 pm and arrives in Thong Sala around 6:00 am next morning, with return trips departing Thong Sala daily at 10:00 pm. The fare is 50 baht for lower deck (straw mat "slave class") and 80 baht for upper deck (pillow and mattress).

It's also possible to purchase a combination train, bus, and ferry ticket from Bangkok's Hualamphong Railway Station directly to Koh Phangan. This includes the train ride to Surat Thani, bus fare from the train station to Ban Don Pier, and the night ferry out to Phangan. Any travel agent in Bangkok with railway ticket service can arrange this itinerary for you.

Koh Phangan is the largest of Samui's neighboring islets and currently has 124 bungalow facilities scattered along its shores. Boats bring tourists from Koh Samui and directly from the mainland.

KOH PHANGAN

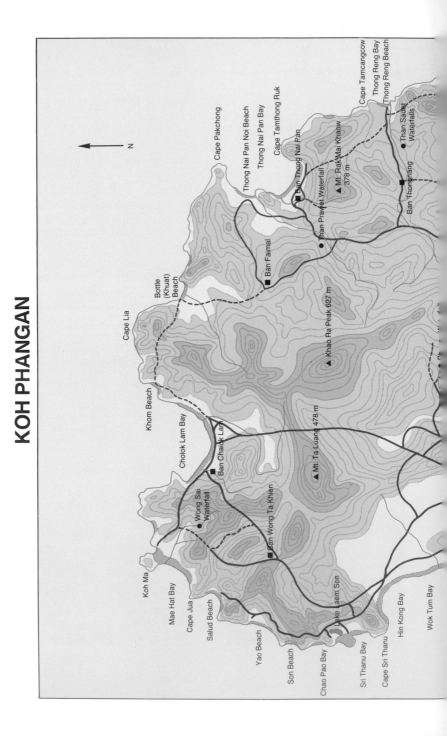

N

Cape Tamcangcow
Thong Reng Bay
Thong Reng Beach

Cape Pakchong
Thong Nai Pan Noi Beach
Thong Nai Pan Bay
Cape Tamthong Ruk
Ban Thong Nai Pan
▲ Mt. Rak Mai Khaow 378 m
Than Sadet Waterfalls
Than Pravet Waterfall
Ban Faimal
Ban Thongnang
Bottle (Khuat) Beach
Cape Lia
▲ Khao Ra Peak 627 m
Khom Beach
Cholok Lam Bay
Ban Chalok Lam
▲ Mt. Ta Luang 478 m
Wong Sai Waterfall
Ban Wong Ta Khien
Koh Ma
Mae Hat Bay
Cape Jua
Salud Beach
Yao Beach
Son Beach
Chao Pao Bay
Sri Thanu Bay
Cape Sri Thanu
Hin Kong Bay
Wok Tum Bay
Lake Laem Son

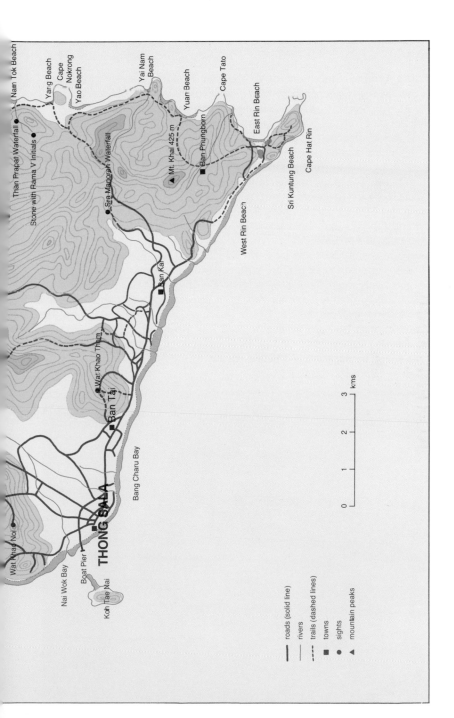

Nam Tok Beach

Yarg Beach

Cape
Nokrong

Yao Beach

Yai Nam
Beach

Than Prapat Waterfall ●

Stone with Rama V Initials ●

Yuan Beach

Sra Mangrah Waterfall

▲ Mt. Khai 425 m

Ban Phungborn ■

Cape Tato

East Rin Beach

Ban Kai ■

West Rin Beach

Sri Kuntung Beach

Cape Hat Rin

Wat Khao Thum ●

Ban Tai ■

Wat Khao Noi ●

Boat Pier ■

THONG SALA

Nai Wok Bay

Bang Charu Bay

Koh Tae Nai

0   1   2   3   kms

—— roads (solid line)
—— rivers
–·–· trails (dashed lines)
■ towns
● sights
▲ mountain peaks

Getting Around Since none of the roads on Koh Phangan are paved, and some of the dirt roads can barely handle even jeeps or motorbikes, the best way to get around the island is by boat. As soon as you arrive at Thong Sala Pier, you'll see fleets of longtail boats bobbing in the water, waiting to run passengers out to various beaches around the island. These boats have signs attached announcing which beaches they service.

From Thong Sala to Hat Rin (Rin Beach), the fare is 30 baht and the ride takes 40 minutes. The boats run whenever a Songserm express boat arrives from Samui. To Yow Beach there is a daily boat service from Thong Sala at 12:00 noon, for 30 baht. From Thong Sala to Thong Nai Pan Bay on the northeast coast there's daily boat service at 12:00 noon January through September only, for 60 baht.

There is also daily boat service from Ban Tai and Ban Kai down to Hat Rin and back, for 20 baht per person, with departures depending on the number of passengers ready to go. To get to secluded Bottle Beach (Hat Khuat) in the north, take a taxi or motorbike to Cholok Lam Bay from Thong Sala, then catch one of the daily boats from there to Bottle Beach at 12:00 noon or 4:00 pm, for 20 baht. Return runs from Bottle Beach go at 9:20 am and 3:20 pm.

You can also arrange your own private boat service from point to point around the island by negotiating a deal with any of the boat men.

By Road Several dirt roads connect Thong Sala to various other points around the island, and taxis make regular runs along these routes. There's a road that cuts due north across the island to Cholok Lam Bay, the fare is 20 baht. Another road runs northwest from Thong Sala to Chao Pao Bay on the west coast, the fare is 15 baht. From Thong Sala east to Ban Tai and Ban Kai the fare is 20 baht, and from Ban Tai northeast to Thong Nai Pan Bay the fare is 60 baht.

Motorcycle taxis also service these routes and generally charge about 10 baht more per person than the *songtao* taxis. Some of the more remote roads can only be traversed by motorbikes, which are also available for rent in Thong Sala for about 150-250 baht per day.

Places on Phangan

Thong Sala This is the only real town on Phangan and the hub of the island's transportation and communications network. A visit here is a must if you wish to change money at bank rates or send or receive mail. Thong Sala also has some travel offices, motorbike rental agencies, a variety of shops, and some restaurants. Beyond these basic services, there is little of interest in the town, except for occasional Thai boxing matches and, from January through June, cock fighting tournaments on Sundays. There are a few bungalows available in and around Thong Sala, but with all the beautiful beaches to choose from, it seems pointless to stay here.

Hat Rin (Rin Beach) souvenir shops. Hat Rin is one of Phangan's most popular hangouts.

Beaches

Koh Phangan is blessed with dozens of attractive beaches and bays, most of which remain largely undeveloped. The majority of the bungalows are concentrated along the southern coast between Thong Sala and Hat Rin, and along the west coast north of Thong Sala, with a few scattered far and wide around the more remote coves of the north and east.

Generally, the nicest white sand beaches are located along the northeast, east, and southeast coastlines. On the other hand, the live coral reefs off the west coast offer excellent snorkeling, and the west coast beaches have greater access to transportation facilities.

The following guide to Koh Phangan's beach scene proceeds eastward along the southern coast from Thong Sala to Hat Rin, then north along the east coast, across the north, and down the west side of the island back to Thong Sala.

Bang Charu Bay This bay stretches from Thong Sala to Ban Thai and has about 15 bungalow facilities scattered along it. The beach itself is medio-cre, but the snorkeling is quite good here, and horseback riding is also available for 200 baht per day. Bungalows run 30-100 baht, and some of the more established names include **Half Moon**, **Coco Club**, and **Charm Beach**.

Beach at Thong Sala Bay in Koh Phangan, which has dozens of attractive beaches and bays, mostly undeveloped.

Ban Tai and Ban Kai These are two small villages located halfway between Thong Sala and Hat Rin. The cross-island road north to Thong Nai Pan Bay on the northeast coast starts at Ban Tai. If all the bungalows are full during peak season of February to June and August September, you can usually rent rooms from local villagers at Ban Kai.

The beaches here are quite nice, with over two dozen hostels to choose from. Very cheap bungalows are available at **Silvery Moon, Boom Cafe**, and **Green Peace** (40-80 baht), and somewhat fancier accommodations at **Lee's Garden** and **Golden Sand Resort** (50-200 baht).

Hat Rin (Rin Beach) This is one of Phangan's most popular hangouts, with direct boat service to and from Bhoput Beach on Samui. It actually consists of two beaches, one on each side of Cape Rin, which sticks out like a thumb from the southeast corner of the island.

The east side of the cape is called Hat Rin Nok (Outer Rin Beach), and it has the best beach. There's good swimming here, as well as good snorkeling along the coral reefs at both ends of the beach, but from October through February the winds sometimes whip the surf up dangerously, so be careful swimming at that time of year. Outer Rin Beach is where the big-bash, all-night, full-moon parties take place each month during the peak seasons, attended by a menagerie of revelers from the island's other beaches as well as from Samui. You'll find inexpensive huts at **Tommy's**, **Hat Rin**, and **Sand Castle** (50-100 baht) and more comfortable accommodations at **Paradise, Palita Lodge**, and **Sun Rise** (60-350 baht). The best food to be found is at Paradise, Hat Rin, and Palita Lodge.

The west side of Cape Rin is called Hat Rin Nai (Inner Rin Beach), and here you'll find a wider selection of bungalows to choose from than the other side of the cape. **Palm Beach** and **Rin Beach** have bungalows ranging from 30 to 200 baht, and way out near the tip of the cape is the scenic located **Light House**, bungalows costing from 80 to 600 baht. There's a flea market here where long-term visitors sell hand embroidered T-shirts, jewelry, coconut shell crafts, and other items.

It doesn't really matter which side of the cape you stay on since it's only a short stroll from one side to the other.

East Coast Capes and Coves Along the east coast between Cape Rin and the next developed beach at Thong Nai Pan Bay lie 18 km (11 miles) of beautiful unspoiled beaches tucked among scenic capes and coves. A dirt trail runs all the way up the coast to Thong Nai Pan Bay, giving access to Hat Yuan (3 km–1.8 miles–from Hat Rin), Hat Yai Nam (4 km–2.5 miles), Hat Yao (5 km–3.1 miles), Hat Yang (6 km–3.8 miles), and Hat Nam Tok (7 km–4.4 m). Here the trail cuts inland to Ban Nam Tok, a small village, then winds another two km (1.2 miles) back to the coast at Thong Reng Bay, which has a lovely beach and a solitary five-bungalow hostel named **No Name** (30-50 baht). From here the trail continues three km (1.8 miles) onward to Thong Nai Pan Bay. Only parts of this coastal trail are negotiable by motorbike, so it's best to walk. If you want to get directly to Thong Nai Pan Bay without walking, take the boat from Hat Rin.

Thong Nai Pan Bay This pretty cove consists of two bays: the lower one called Thong Ta Pan Yai (Big Thong Ta Pan) and the upper one Thong Ta Pan Noi (Little Thong Ta Pan). There are six hostels on Big Thong Ta Pan Bay, with bungalows ranging in price from 30 to 200 baht. Daily jeep service (weather and road conditions permitting) is available from the village on this bay, Ban Thong Nai Pan.

Up around the headland which divides the two bays, overlooking Little Thong Ta Pan, is a very pleasant place called **Panviman Resort**, with 50 bungalows that rent for 200-1,200 baht. This is a bit expensive by Phangan standards, but the facilities and scenic location certainly justify the cost. If you're looking for something cheaper and more rustic, try the **Thong Ta Pan Resort** further up the beach, with 18 bungalows going for 60-150 baht.

Bottle Beach (Hat Khuat) Aficionados of Koh Phangan rate Bottle Beach as one of the most enchanting hideaways on the island. Tucked along a secluded cove on the northern shore, it can be reached by hiking three km (1.8 miles) along an island trail from Thong Nai Pan, or by taking a boat from Cholok Lam Bay to the west. There are three no-frills bungalow facilities here: the original **Bottle Beach**, the **Sea Love**, and the dubiously named **O.D.** Rates ranges between 40 and 80 baht for a hut.

Cholok Lam Bay This is a large, attractive bay with several nice beaches on it. On the east end, enveloped in its own cove, is **Khom Beach**, where you can rent a rustic hut for 40-50 baht at either **Coral Bay** or **Suan Hin**. Further west along the main beach are several more facilities with slightly better bungalows going for 50-200 baht. At the village of Ban Cholok Lam you can shop for basic provisions and catch taxis back to Thong Sala.

Mae Hat Bay Continuing westward around the headland you'll come to Mae Hat Bay, which has a mediocre beach but some good snorkeling along the coastal coral reefs and around the offshore islet of **Koh Ma**. There are several hostels on this beach, the best of which seems to be **Island View Cabana**, with bungalows costing 100-250 baht per night and a fairly good restaurant. There's also a small village, Ban Mae Hat, located three km (1.8 miles) from Ban Cholok Lam and accessible by taxi or motorbike.

Return to Lotusland

I had been away for two years when I returned to the island last month (August, 1982) with a New Zealander friend, who teaches in Songkhla. This time the trip up from Songkhla was pure luxury: two hours by taxi to Nakhon Si Thammarat, another hour and a half to Khanom and the new ferry. Well, not so new. It's nineteen years old, a dowager from Japan who has managed to age gracefully into shabby gentility. There are indoor fountains and plastic gardens, couches to lounge or sleep upon, plastic bucket seats on the fantail where one can spread one's legs, sip a beer and watch the boat's wake churn away. Passage to Koh Samui is now a mere 90 minutes. The special pier for the ferry, located several miles south of the main harbor, boasts a modern motel-and-restaurant complex. The paved road around Koh Samui has long been completed and we were whisked rapidly and comfortably back to the original bungalow on Chawang Beach (named, naturally enough, "First Bungalow"). The old red clapboard building is still there, but the number of shoreline bungalows has tripled and what used to be a thatch-roofed hut of a restaurant is now a spacious, L-shaped, high-ceilinged, balustraded, carved wood-and-bamboo pavilion, which seats well over a hundred diners. The menu has changed too: cheeseburgers, steaks, spaghetti, wiener schnitzel...

A walk on the beach on the next day brought more suprises. There are a half-dozen windsurfers for rent, a paperback rental library featuring books in five languages, and even an open-air disco. Bungalows, greatly enlarged and prettified, come equipped now with indoor toilets and wrap-around verandahs. Some are large enough to pass as American-style motel units. The architectural style of one double-decker boutique-cum-fern bar of white stucco and polished pine—"The Malibu"—was pure Hollywood Modern. The invasion of this sort of seashell-and-fishing-net kitsch depresses me. Must every pristine beach in the world fall prey to Californication?

The guests at these bungalows have changed too. They are still young and they come from the same places. Enter any restaurant and you can hear German, Swedish, Danish, Dutch, Aussie twang and, this being August, a great deal of French and Italian. But what happened to all the freaks? *No more nose rings or silver anklets or floursack sarongs. Oh, out on the beach you can still find plenty of barebreasted teutonic amazons to ogle at, but in the restaurants everyone wears the sort of spiffy casual-wear you can find at any Mediterranean resort. The bungalow dwellers of Koh Samui now seem to be young profession-*

*als, students, married couples who fly out to Asia for a month's vacation—
not the hard-core world-travelling freaks of old. In fact, the only beard-and-
long-hair I saw on the beach belonged to an Australian, who, when asked,
gave his occupation as "biker". He seemed strangely out of place, though,
amid all the cropped heads and clean-shaven faces.*

*After a good many beers one night my New Zealander friend, who has
been to Koh Samui a dozen times, waxed philosophical: "The way to
understand the phenomenon of Koh Samui is to look at it from the local's
point of view. Tourism is a kind of agrobusiness. Koh Samui used to be
famous for its coconuts, but since the bottom of the copra market dropped
out, people here have switched to raising* farangs.*"*

"Huh?"

*"Sure. Like cattle. You rent them a stall and you set them out to pasture
on the beach and three times a day these huge* farangs *come shambling and
mooing into your restaurant to gobble and swill to their heart's content. And
like guernsey cows they produce a steady and copious steam of money."*

*The analogy made sense to me. A perfect symbiotic relationship. The
travellers want a peaceful, quiet beach; the locals need cash. My only worry
is that one day this equilibrium will be shattered. Large first class hotels are
going up in Surat Thani, which now advertizes itself as the "Gateway to Koh
Samui". Already on Bo Put Beach there is a major complex of air-
conditioned motel suites catering to wealthy tourists. The First Bungalow
is beginning to prepare ground for "modern accommodations", which will
house busloads of Bangkok tourists coming over on the Khanom ferry. How
much longer before the first Holiday Inn high-rise rears its ugly head?*

*Another analogy comes to mind. The freaks, the wild-and-woolly world
travellers, are often the pioneers of tourism, the ones to first explore places
like Penang's Batu Ferringi and Phuket's Patong Beach. Later the promot-
ers and tour operators and hotel chains move in, "civilizing" and irrevocably
changing the exotic locales they were supposed to be capitalizing upon.*

*Don't get me wrong. Chawang Beach is still gorgeous, virtually
untouched. But if you want to see it, don't wait too long. The beach has
changed amazingly in five years. In another five or ten, it might not be there
anymore. In which ase leave Koh Samui and move on to Koh Phangan, a
smaller island ten miles to the north. I suspect that's where all the freaks have
gone.*

James Eckardt, Waylaid by the Bimbos, *Post Publishing Co 1991*

Salud, Yao, and Son Beach Between Mae Hat and Chao Pao Bay five km (3.1 miles) to the south are three coves with rather uninspiring beaches called "Salud," "Yao," and "Son." But since there are ten bungalow facilities strung along this stretch of the island, these beaches must have their own attractions, such as snorkeling and beautiful sunsets over the sea.

Chao Pao Bay Chao Pao Bay is usually lumped together with neighboring **Sri Thanu Bay**, although a cape actually separates them. You'll find extensive coral reefs offshore, good for snorkeling, and an inland lake behind the cape. There is a selection of nine bungalow facilities, the most comfortable of which is **Loy Fah**, with 25 cabins ranging in price from 50 to 300 baht.

Wok Tum Bay This is a big bay with little to recommend it except plenty of open beach and some fairly good spots for snorkeling and scuba diving. On the north side sits a solitary hostel called **Lipstick** (30-100 baht), and near the southern headland are **Tuk**, **Kiet**, and **O.K.**, with similar rates.

Nai Wok Bay The beach here is just a short stroll from Thong Sala, in case you wish to stay near town, but that's about its only advantage. There are ten hostels to choose from, ranging from 30 to 300 baht per night, including two located up on the hill behind the beach.

Tae Nai Island This islet sits about one km off the Thong Sala Pier and has one 17-bungalow facility with huts renting for 150-200 baht. There's not much to do there, but some people like the feeling of living on a deserted island, like Robinson Crusoe. There's daily boat service from Thong Sala to Tae Nai at 12:00 noon and 5:00 pm, for a fare of 5 baht.

Inland Sights

Koh Phangan is a mostly mountainous island, with its highest point, Khao Ra, rising to 627 meters (2,069 feet). The mountains are ribboned with fast streams that form some nice waterfalls, and there are numerous hiking trails leading to various scenic viewpoints.

Waterfalls Five km (3.1 miles) north of Thong Sala, off the road to Cholok Lam, you'll find **Phaeng Waterfall**, which looks its best during or immediately after the rainy season.

About halfway up the road from Ban Thai to Thong Nai Pan there's a turnoff heading east towards Sadet Beach. This trail follows a river along which you'll see a series of waterfalls collectively known as the **Than Sadet Waterfalls**. Than Sadet is also a historical site due to frequent visits there between 1888 and 1909 by Siam's great King Chulalongkorn, Rama V, whose initials

are engraved on two big boulders along this rocky river. King Rama VII also left his initials on some stones there in 1926 and 1930, and more recently, in 1962, the current reigning monarch King Bhumipol (Rama IX) followed his illustrious predecessors' footsteps and engraved his own initials on a stone. This is an interesting area to explore on foot.

There are several other waterfalls around the island, including **Than Prapat** near the east coast beach of Hat Nam Tok, **Than Prawet** about two km (1.2 miles) inland from Thong Nai Pan Bay (where King Rama V also left his initials engraved in stone), and **Wong Sai** up in the island's northwest corner about one km inland from Mae Hat Bay.

Mountain View Points Khao Ra (Mount Ra) is the highest point on the island at 627 meters (2,069 feet), and there is a long winding foot trail that leads up to this scenic vantage point from the village of **Ban Madua Wan**, located about four km (2.5 miles) north of Thong Sala on the road to Cholok Lam. The trail is steep and often treacherous, so travelers are advised to take advantage of the guide service available at Ban Madua Wan, where for 200-300 baht, the village chief will assign a guide to lead you up the trail.

About one km east of Phaeng Waterfall is another mountain view point accessible by foot, and up in the northwest, at the village of Ban Wong Ta Khien, there is a 1.5 km (1 mile) trail leading to a scenic point and waterfall on Mt. Ta Luang. There's a more easily accessible mountain view point in the southwest corner of Phangan near Hat Rin, along a foot path that branches north off the northern trail connecting the eastern and western beaches of Hat Rin.

Wat Khao Tham On top of a steep hill near the village of Ban Tai on the southern coast is a scenic cave temple called **Wat Khao Tham**, where for many years an American monk lived and meditated. His ashes are still there, entombed on a steep bluff below the temple. Wayfarers may stay overnight at this Buddhist retreat, but facilities are extremely basic, and you'll have to haul your own food and supplies from the village below. Needless to say, this is not a place to party, but if you practice meditation, a few days sojourn here might do you some good. Occasionally, monks organize ten-day meditation retreats, and anyone with the discipline to practice is welcome to participate.

Koh Tao ("Turtle Island")

If Koh Phangan is 15 years behind Samui in development, then Koh Tao is in a different era altogether. Known as "Turtle Island" due to its shape, the pace of life here is just about as slow and unhurried as its namesake. More remote and pristine than either Samui or Phangan, Koh Tao has much the same feeling of seclusion and self-containment that Goa and Phuket did when first "discovered" by latter day Marco Polos in the early 1970s.

A small island of only 21 sq. km (8.1 sq. miles), located some 47 km (30 miles) north of Koh Phangan, and with a resident population of about 750 persons, Koh Tao's shores are stacked with huge boulders baked golden brown by the sun and polished smooth by wind and water. Viewed from various angles at different times of the day, these massive stone sculptures suggest all sorts of exotic images to the eye.

The island relies almost entirely on coconuts for its economic welfare, and you can still see stout, sarong-clad women preparing coconuts for copra production the old-fashioned way by roasting the split ripe nuts over big slow-burning charcoal fires. The aroma is sweet and musky, and you can buy small bottles of the freshly extracted oil at village shops for only 10 baht. It's a great emollient for skin and hair baked dry by the sun.

A fishing boat typical of those that ply the waters between Koh Tao and Koh Samui.

KOH TAO

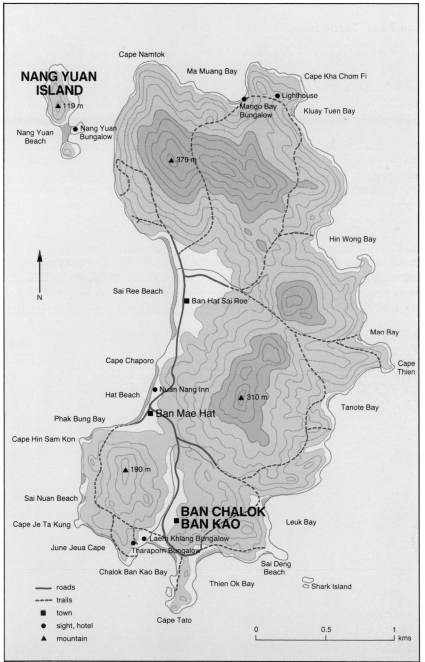

NANG YUAN
ISLAND

▲119 m

Nang Yuan
Beach

● Nang Yuan
Bungalow

Cape Namtok

Ma Muang Bay

Cape Kha Chom Fi

● Lighthouse

Mango Bay
Bungalow

Kluay Tuen Bay

▲379 m

Hin Wong Bay

N

Sai Ree Beach

■ Ban Hat Sai Ree

Mao Bay

Cape Chaporo

Cape
Thien

Hat Beach

● Nuan Nang Inn

▲310 m

Phak Bung Bay

■ Ban Mae Hat

Tanote Bay

Cape Hin Sam Kon

▲190 m

Sai Nuan Beach

Cape Je Ta Kung

■ BAN CHALOK
■ BAN KAO

Leuk Bay

June Jeua Cape

● Laem Khlang Bungalow
Tharaporn Bungalow

Chalok Ban Kao Bay

Sai Deng
Beach

Thien Ok Bay

〜 Shark Island

—— roads
--- trails
■ town
● sight, hotel
▲ mountain

Cape Tato

0   0.5   1
⌞—————————⌟ kms

Owing to its distance from the mainland as well as from Samui and Phangan, Koh Tao does not get swamped by day-trippers on weekends and holidays. There's little point in going there for just a day, unless you want to spend the entire day bobbing back and forth on a boat. Even if you're visiting from Phangan, which is three hours away, you should plan to spend at least a night or two on Koh Tao in order to get a feel for the place and let it work its magic on you.

Getting There

Koh Tao may not be reached directly from Koh Samui, but must be approached via Koh Phangan, 47 km (30 miles) journey, north of Phangan. There's a daily boat from Thong Sala on Koh Phangan to Ban Mae Hat on Koh Tao at 12:00 noon, with return trips departing Koh Tao daily at 8:00 am. The fare is 100 baht, and the trip takes 3-4 hours. During peak season (January-March) Songserm Travel operates express boats from Thong Sala to Ban Mae Hat daily at 9:30 am, returning at 2:00 am. The fare is 200 baht, and the trip takes two hours.

You can also reach Koh Tao directly from the Tha Yang Pier near the town of Chumphon, located about 100 km (62 miles) north of Surat Thani on the mainland. Boats depart about four times a week, and the six-hour ride costs 150 baht. If you opt for this route and are coming from Bangkok, be sure to book your train ticket only as far as Chumphon, not all the way to Surat Thani. If you are with a sufficiently large party or have plenty of money to spend, it may be worthwhile chartering a boat of your own to run you from Chumphon to Koh Tao. You should be able to negotiate the trip for 2,500-3,000 baht one-way.

Note that all boat service to and from Koh Tao depends on weather and sea conditions and is therefore subject to last minute delay or cancellation. If that happens to you, remember the old Thai maxim *chai-yen*, "Be patient."

Getting Around From the main village of Ban Mae Hat on the west coast there is a dirt road branching north to the village and beach of Ban Hat Ree and south to Chalok Ban Kao and Thanok Bay. All other trails are negotiable by foot only. A few *songtao* taxis and motorbikes ply the two roads, and sometimes you can rent motorbikes at Ban Mae Hat, but it makes more sense to hike around on foot. Most beaches and bays are less than two km (1.2 miles) apart.

From Ban Mae Hat you can also hire private boats to take you to any beach on the island, or on a complete round-the-island tour.

Places

Ban Mae Hat This is the main village and landing point for all inter-island boats. Here you'll find a few dockside restaurants, some diving shops, and a few stores selling produce and provisions. You can also change money, post letters, and make long-distance calls in the village.

There are a few bungalow facilities within walking distance of the village, including **Nuan Nang** just north of town. This is a reliable resort with bungalows going for 50-100 baht and fairly good food.

Beaches and Bays

Koh Tao features particularly good scuba diving and snorkeling along its offshore coral reefs, and the beaches are also excellent for swimming and sun bathing. There is some good fishing a bit further offshore. Koh Tao currently has two dozen bungalow facilities, most of them along the western and southern coasts.

Moving counter clockwise around the island from Ban Mae Hat, here's a brief guide to the best beaches and bays.

The shores of Koh Tao are stacked with huge boulders, baked golden brown by the sun and polished smooth by wind and water.

Sai Nuan Beach Located about two km (1.2 miles) south of Ban Mae Hat, this beach is accessible only by the coastal foot trail. It has three hostels with simple huts going for 50-80 baht, plus another one scenically situated up on the promontory at Cape Hin Sam Kon.

Chalok Ban Kao Bay Two km (1.2 miles) east of Sai Nuan is a beautiful bay with two beaches and six hostels. You can reach Chalok Ban Kao by foot on a trail from Sai Nuan, or by dirt road directly from Ban Mae Hat.
At **Tharaporn** and **Laem Khlang** you'll find basic huts for 50-80 baht. This bay is particularly good for snorkeling, especially along the southern shoreline at Cape Tato, which has some impressive rock formations.

Thien Ok Bay On the east side of Cape Tato lies another set of pretty beaches facing onto Thien Ok Bay, where there are four hostels ranging in price from 40 to 100 baht. About 1/2 km off Sai Daeng Beach floats tiny **Shark Island**, which is reputed to be infested with sharks, although there have been no reports of any attacks on divers or swimmers. Thai sharks are probably too laid-back and too well fed to bother people.

Leuk Bay Around the cape, tucked into a scenic cove on the southwest corner of the island, is lovely Leuk Bay, which has a couple of small hostels with huts renting for 40-60 baht. This is one of the most attractive bays on Koh Tao, and even if you don't stay here, it makes for a great side-trip by boat or foot from Ban Mae Hat or other nearby beaches.

East Coast Bays Two km (1.2 miles) north of Leuk Bay is **Tanote Bay**, with two simple facilities, and a further one km north of that is **Cape Thien**, with one facility. Next comes **Mao Bay**, then there's a long stretch of empty shoreline until you reach **Hin Wong Bay**, a beautiful cove on the northeast coast, with one hostel. Around the headland above Hin Wong are **Kluay Tuen Bay** and **Cape Kha Chom Fi**, where you'll find some great scuba and snorkeling waters but no accommodations as of this writing.

Ma Muang (Mango) Bay Located on the narrow northern coast, Mango Bay is another good snorkeling and diving area, and here you can find cheap accommodations (30-50 baht) at the **Mango Bay**.

Nam Tok and Sai Ree Beach Around the northwest headland of Cape Nam Tok, down along the northwest coast, is a long stretch of beach called Nam Tok, with four hostels. Nam Tok runs southward and becomes Sai Ree Beach, which has two bungalow facilities and a small village. At the southern headland of Sai Ree Beach is Cape Chaporo, where **Khao Inn** offers bungalows for 50 baht. South of that you're back at Ban Mae Hat.

Nang Yuan Island

Located one km off the northwest coast of Koh Tao sits exotic "Nang Yuan Island," literally "The Isle of the Seated Barbarian." It actually consists of three tiny islets all connected by a strip of beach, perhaps the only such "tri-island" beach in the world. There's a bungalow facility here called **Nang Yuan**, with about two dozen bungalows going for 80-200 baht. The snorkeling along the shores and shallow bays of this triplet isle ranks among the best in the Gulf of Thailand, but try to avoid going there when big groups of divers come in by boat from Phangan and Samui. There's only so much space to explore here and it can get awfully crowded when 100 people are swimming around.

Even if you're not into snorkeling and don't want to stay on this islet, it's definitely worth a visit if you find yourself on Koh Tao. Boats run out there daily from Ban Mae Hat at 10:00 am, returning at 4:30 pm, for a 10-baht fare.

Nang Yuan Island consists of three small islets connected together by narrow strips of beach.

122

Anthong National Marine Park is an enchanting wonderland of bulbous green isles, clear blue lagoons, mysterious caves, and exotic rock formations.

Anthong National Marine Park

31 km (19 miles) northwest of Koh Samui lies the 50-isle archipelago of Anthong National Marine Park, an enchanting wonderland of bulbous green isles, clear blue lagoons, mysterious caves, and exotic rock formations. Anthong is the primary spawning grounds for Thailand's much beloved *pla thoo*, a sort of mackerel which appears in all sorts of Thai dishes, hence the archipelago's name, "Golden Basin."

Approaching Anthong by boat is like entering one of those dreamy classical Chinese landscape paintings, with the islands rising from the sea in the traditional "Dragon Ridge" mountain motif, mist clinging to peaks, sea and sky lines merging hazily on the horizon, billowing white clouds stacked like piles of fleece in the sky. Rocky crags and green turrets jut abruptly at odd angles from these islets, etching all sorts of suggestive shapes against the sky.

Koh Mae (Mother Island) features a miniature beach surrounded by towering walls of craggy cliffs. This turquoise-colored lake looks like a tropical fantasy.

The islands range in size from that of Koh Tao to mere bumps on the water, and they are riddled with dozens of hidden coves and caves, splashed with white sand beaches, and surrounded by crystal clear lagoons. The main island **Koh Nua Ta Lap** (Isle of the Sleeping Cow) has a bungalow facility that costs 250 baht per night, including three meals. **Koh Mae** (Mother Island) features a miniature beach surrounded by towering walls of craggy cliffs that look like a set for a science fiction film. Some of the beach coves on the smaller islands are so picture perfect that they seem like tropical fantasies.

There's a boat that runs daily from Nathon on Samui out to Anthong at 8:30 am, returning the same day at 5:00 pm. The fare is 200-250 baht per person round-trip, including lunch and a tour of the islands. Songserm Travel, Samui Travel Center, and Highway Travel also operate regularly scheduled tours to An Thong, frequency depending on the time of year and weather conditions. You can also arrange private excursions through some of the hotels. This is a worthwhile side trip and should not be missed if you're spending a week or so on Koh Samui.

Tourists could spend weeks exploring the beautiful seas and islands in the area.

Sports and Recreation

If simply romping in the sun and surf does not suffice to keep you entertained, Koh Samui offers a variety of marine sports and other recreational activities to help pass the time.

Snorkeling and Scuba Diving Snorkeling and scuba are probably the most rewarding aquatic activities in and around Samui. Although pollution has killed off many of Samui's own offshore coral reefs, there are still a few capes and coves around the island worth exploring underwater. The best of these are the reefs off Cape Sor in the southwest corner, the waters off the rocky shores of Coral Cove between Chaweng and Lamai, and the extensive coral reefs at Bang Po Bay along the northeast coast. Dedicated aficionados, however, will want to join the regularly scheduled diving and snorkeling excursions out to Koh Tao and Anthong National Marine Park for some of the most superb submarine scenery in Southeast Asia.

If you're not a certified scuba diver but wish to learn, there are numerous certified diving schools in Koh Samui offering both PADI and NAUI professional courses. Some of the bigger outfits are listed below:

Koh Samui Divers This is the oldest scuba operation on Samui. You'll find their head office on Anthong Road in Nathon (Tel & Fax 421-465), and a branch office at the Malibu Beach Club on Chaweng Beach (Tel 421-386).

They also have a fully equipped dive center opposite the pier at Ban Mae Hat on Koh Tao.

Swiss International Dive Center Head office in Nathon, across the street from the Golden Lion, with a branch at Coral Cove.

Matlang Divers 67/2 Watana Rd in Nathon, with branch facilities at North Chaweng.

Samui International Diving School Nathon

Seafantasea Nathon, with a branch facility at the Sea Fan resort on Maenam Beach

Diving Today On Route 4169 in Ban Lamai

In addition to these professional diving organizations, some bungalows offer private snorkeling and scuba excursions for their guests, and if their boats are not fully booked, non-guests are usually welcome to sign aboard. You'll find excellent excursions available at Ziggy Stardust on Bophut Beach, Poppies on Chaweng, and the Imperial Tong Sai Bay on Choeng Mon, as well as a few other resorts around the island.

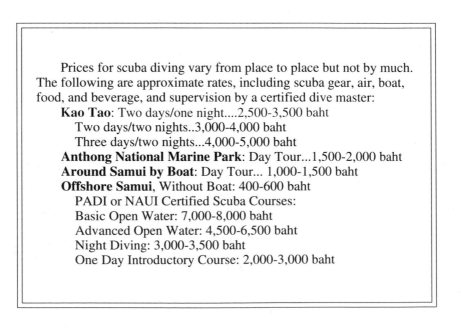

Prices for scuba diving vary from place to place but not by much. The following are approximate rates, including scuba gear, air, boat, food, and beverage, and supervision by a certified dive master:

Kao Tao: Two days/one night....2,500-3,500 baht
Two days/two nights..3,000-4,000 baht
Three days/two nights...4,000-5,000 baht
Anthong National Marine Park: Day Tour...1,500-2,000 baht
Around Samui by Boat: Day Tour... 1,000-1,500 baht
Offshore Samui, Without Boat: 400-600 baht
PADI or NAUI Certified Scuba Courses:
Basic Open Water: 7,000-8,000 baht
Advanced Open Water: 4,500-6,500 baht
Night Diving: 3,000-3,500 baht
One Day Introductory Course: 2,000-3,000 baht

Surfing The only beaches with good waves for board or body surfing are Chaweng and Lamai on the east coast. Most other beaches and bays around the island don't have shore-breaking waves.

Depending on prevailing winds and tides, you can wind surf almost anywhere around Koh Samui, Koh Phagnan, and Koh Tao. On Samui, the best wind surfing conditions are usually found at Chaweng, Lamai, Bophut, and Maenam.

Boating and Fishing There are power boats for rent by the hour and the day on all the Big Six beaches of Samui. These boats can take you out on the open sea for fishing or zoom you around the bays for water skiing. Some bungalows have their own boats for hire, as do all diving outfits. The lodge on Bophut and Poppies on Chaweng have a big power boat as well as a nice sailing catamaran, and Ziggy Stardust on Bophut has a comfortable Chinese sailing junk for excursions around Samui and out to neighboring islands. On Chaweng and Lamai you'll also find power boats specializing in the high-flying aqua-aerial sport of parasailing. Rates vary, but you can expect to pay 350-500 per hour or 1,000-2,000 per day for a boat, depending on its size and condition, the services required, and the number of people on board.

Fishing boats, power boats, even a Chinese sailing junk, are available on Koh Samui. You can also arrange private boating excursions on Koh Phangan and Koh Tao with fishermen and longtail boat operators.

You can also arrange private boating excursions at Thong Sala on Koh Phagnan and Ban Mae Hat on Koh Tao by negotiating a deal with fishermen and commercial longtail boat operators, but be sure to take a careful look at the condition of the boat as well as the boat man before shelling out any money. On the outer islands, the best way to get a reliable boat and helmsman is to inquire at the local diving shops, restaurants, and hostels.

Go-Cart Racing Joy riders may find some thrills at the **Samui Kart Club**, located on Route 4169 across from the Samui Euphoria resort at Bophut. It's open daily from 10:00 am until 6:30 pm and costs 200 baht for a ten-minute spin. It has a good track built beneath the shade of a coconut grove, and some of the carts can speed up to 90 kph, so be careful.

Thai Boxing (*Muay Thai*) There are several Thai boxing rings on Koh Samui, including one on the northern outshirts of Nathon and one at the Flamingo complex in Lamai. Consult your bungalow manager or the local "Samui Today" newspaper for scheduled bouts. There's also a Thai boxing ring at Thong Sala on Koh Phangan.

The Flamingo in Lamai offers a training program in this pugilistic art, and if you're feeling pugnacious, you can climb into the ring and test your skills against a real Thai boxer. *Farang* challengers have been known to win these no-holds-barred bouts, but not very often.

Samui Kart Club offers go-cart racing beneath the shade of a coconut grove.

Buffalo Fighting In the past, Koh Samui was known for a distinctive sporting event called "Buffalo Fighting." Not to be confused with Spanish bull fighting, this event pits two water buffalos in a corral, for a gouging, lock-horned battle. You can still see signs pointing to the dilapidated rings all around Samui.

However, in early 1991, the governor of Surat Thani province, who has jurisdiction over Samui, decreed a ban on buffalo fights when he discovered that local spectators had turned this traditional pastime into a major gambling operation. Currently, the only exception to this prohibition is during the annual festivities celebrating traditional Thai New Year (*Songkran*) in April, but like all prohibitions it may not last long, so if this sort of spectacle appeals to you, ask around and you might find a match.

Although "Buffalo Fighting" was banned in early 1991, it is still part of the Songkran festivities in April on Koh Samui.

Hiking Two-thirds of Samui consists of steep green mountains, and trekkers will find plenty of trails to satisfy their wanderlust. Among the best hikes in Samui are the ones from Lamai up to Overlap Stone and beyond to Samui Hin (465 meters–1,535 feet) and then from Samui Hin to the southern trail across the road from Wat Khunaram and the Hin Lat Waterfall. There are other longer hiking trails, but for those it's best to take along an experienced local guide.

Koh Phangan also has some great mountain trails, such as the hike up to the highest peak at Khao Ra (627 meters–2,069 ft), the walk along the river and falls at Than Sadet, and the trail to Ta Luand Waterall in the northwest. Most of these can be safely done alone, but you should hire a guide at Ban Madua Wan for the hike up to Khao Ra.

Koh Tao is small enough to hike across the entire length and width of the island in a single day, and none of the trails take you higher than 350 meters (1,155 feet), so all you need is a good pair of walking shoes and a sufficient supply of drinking water.

Festivals All the popular traditional Thai festivals are celebrated with colorful pomp and ceremony on Koh Samui, including *Songkran* (Thai New Year) on April 13th, *Visakha Bucha* (the day of the Buddha's birth, enlightenment, and death) full moon of May, *Loy Krathong* (in honor of Mae Khongkha, goddess of rivers and waterways) full moon of November, and others. In addition, there's a special local "Samui Festival" held each year, usually between April and June, featuring contests among coconut picking monkeys, beer drinking contests for men, beauty contests for ladies, and other carnival theatrics.

Health Holidays

How many times have you gone on a holiday only to return home feeling more exhausted and distressed than when you left? The impulse to "eat, drink, and be merry" and to party till you drop is deeply ingrained in the holiday travel circuit, and most resorts actively encourage such senseless behavior with all sorts of enticing temptations, for which they charge a premium to boot!

In recent years, a new wind has begun to blow through the holiday travel world, sowing the seeds of a new vacation concept–the "Health Holiday." Instead of spending a lot of precious time and money further depleting one's energy and eroding one's health, the idea is to take advantage of holiday time to recharge one's bio-batteries, replenish vitality, and restore health. Indulging in excessive food and drink once or twice a week, or staying up all night howling at the moon once in a while, is fine, but driving yourself to the outer limits of endurance day and night makes about as much sense as banging your head against a brick wall.

Holiday health resorts have already sprouted up in France, Hawaii, Australia, and, surprisingly, Russia, plus a few other places, but the concept remains relatively new in Asia. As recent prosperity unleashes waves of unbridled self-indulgence in the Far East, along with all its attendant health hazards, the idea of using leisure time to restore health is beginning to take root in Asia as well. In Thailand, a

Therapeutic massage is widely practiced throughout Thailand. There's no better investment than the nimble healing hands of experienced Thai massage therapists.

few far-sighted entrepreneurs are now beginning to establish holiday health resorts to cater to the casualties of modern life in the fast lane.

Phuket and Pattaya have already been developed entirely as playground resorts, and Bangkok is so polluted and profligate that locating health centers there would be like trying to diet in a pastry shop, but Koh Samui has just the right balance of ambiance and attitude for the health holiday concept, and this is where the idea is taking root in Thailand. Hopefully it will spread to the hills of the north as well.

The idea is simple: you check into a comfortable bungalow in a tranquil resort, far away from the worries and burdens of home and office, and instead of spending day and night in the throes of "Saturday Night Fever," you systematically relax, detoxify, and rejuvenate body and mind with therapeutic massage, herbal steam baths, nutritional and herbal supplements, wholesome food, and other restorative programs. You don't even have to stay at an actual health resort: all you have to do is stay within reach of one and avail yourself of its facilities.

One of the early pioneers of health spas in Samui, Dr. Sukoom, is the proprietor of the **Garden Home Herbal Health Center**, located two km (1.25 miles) north of Nathon on Route 4169 (Tel 421-311). In addition to traditional Thai therapeutic massage (150 baht), Dr. Sukoom has developed a highly effective detoxifying herbal steam bath (250 baht), using the popular "New Age pyramid" design to concentrate vital energy inside the steam room. Hot herbal steam is piped into the pyramids, where patients lie down and absorb the essence via the skin and lungs thereby driving toxins out of the body. The cleansing effect is swift and tangible. He also brews a variety of therapeutic teas prepared with herbs grown on Koh Samui. He blends potent herbal oils for massage and skin care. Garden Home is open daily from 9:00 am till 5:00 pm, and health enthusiasts will find it well worth a visit. The herbal steam is great therapy for hangovers!

Across the island in Upper Lamai, next door to the Rose Garden bungalows, is a similar health center called **Herbal Home**, which also offers Thai massage and herbal steam baths, as well as special physical and herbal therapy for specific individual ailments. The regular combination steam and massage runs 300 baht, while fees for special treatments vary according to individual conditions.

Dr. Sukoom

At the **Fair House** in Little
Chaweng, just south of the
headland from Central
Chaweng, is another Thai
massage and herbal steam
facility called, fair enough, Fair
Health. And at the **Koh Samui
Intercultural Center** near the
hospital south of Nathon, you
can arrange to take private or
group courses in yoga and
meditation under the tutelage of
old Samui hands Greg and
Hillary Hitt.

Meanwhile, Samui's first
fully equipped, all-inclusive
health spa is currently under
development at Longevity
Beach in Upper Lamai at the
Island Spa and Resort and
should be in operation by early
1992. Dream-child of American

*Dr. Sukoom's "New Age Pyramid"
steam room*

expat Guy Hopkins, a former denizen of Bangkok who finally saw the
light, the Island Spa plans to install a wide range of health and recreational facilities, including Thai massage, herbal steam, jacuzzi, a
therapeutic fasting and detoxification program, tennis courts, swimming pool, gym, health juice bar, and more, all within the context of a
holiday beach resort with private bungalows. Non-residents who
choose to stay elsewhere may still use the spa facilities at special half-
day and full-day rates, and there are annual memberships available
entitling frequent visitors to discounts on everything from accommodations to health services.

In addition to these facilities, there are many simple no-frills Thai
massage centers around the island, including a few in Nathon, and
there's no better investment in all of Thailand than the few hundred
baht to rent the nimble healing hands of experienced Thai massage
therapists. Try it, and have a healthy holiday!

The Samui Scene

Koh Samui may be approached on two different levels, depending on how you like to travel. On the one hand, you can make all travel arrangements through a travel agent, stay at a big international style resort, and participate only in scheduled events and group tours on and around the island. This approach makes for a simple, hassle-free visit and costs more than the "on-your-own" approach, but it also renders your sojourn on Samui little different from any other tropical island resort.

The other way is to go it alone and make your own arrangements, select your own personal preference in accommodations, and explore Samui and its neighboring islands yourself. This requires a bit of effort and inevitably involves some trial-and-error tactics, but for intrepid travelers who seek an "in-depth experience" wherever they go, the independent approach will open up the doors to the uniquely local "Samui Scene."

What distinguishes the Samui Scene from other resort islands? It's a combination of native island charm and certain traditions brought to Samui by travelers escaping from the excessive commercialization of other resorts around Asia. Samui's own customs speak for themselves, so let's take a look at some of the lifestyles transplanted here from elsewhere.

Koh Samui, and particularly Koh Phangan and Koh Tao, have fallen heir to many of the grand traditions fostered during the "Golden Age" of travel in Goa and Bali during the late 60s and early 70s. As Goa and Bali and many similar points in between try to cash in on up-market tourism by imitating the Riviera and Waikiki, they have elbowed aside and given short shrift to the hippies and backpackers who first discovered them and eventually brought them to the world's attention. As a result, these old-timers have wandered far and wide in search of new waters, and during the early 80s they discovered Koh Samui and her neighboring isles.

Samui was perfect. Here the grand Thai traditions of *sanuk* (fun) and *sabai* (comfort) manifested themselves as the guiding principles of island life. Unlike Phuket and Pattaya, Samui had not been over-built and over-priced by greedy commercial developers. It stood aloof from the rest of the world. It was beautiful. Today, these conditions still largely prevail, despite the rapid pace of development, and with a bit of luck, foresight, and balanced planning, the Samui Scene might just survive and flourish indefinitely.

The all-night beach parties which happen each month under the full moon in Samui, Phangan, and Tao are examples of a tradition transplanted root, trunk, and blossom from the shores of Goa and Bali. The alfresco flea market on Koh Phangan is another example, and indeed old Goa hands will no doubt recognize some of the craftsmen and vendors there. There's also a growing community of visitors who come back year after year and stay on for month after month, just as they used to do in Goa and Bali prior to the barbaric onslaught of mass tourism. Within this community you'll find an open-minded attitude of international fellowship that any traveler can depend upon for companionship and direction. But you cannot ask a travel agent to arrange it: you have to reach out on your own to get it.

Popular Hangouts One of the best ways to meet venerable veterans of the Samui Scene is to frequent the popular hangouts they favor. In Nathon, for example, you might have a few drinks and a snack at the **Golden Lion** or the **Bird in Hand** and keep your eyes and ears peeled for interesting characters. At Chaweng, you're bound to meet some old Samui hands if you hang around the **Jazz Bar** and the **Wild Orchid Cafe**. At **Poppies** you'll find some refugees from the Bali Scene. The Ibiza crowd likes to hang out at **The Island**, and **Munchies** often attracts a mixed bag of characters.

Over on Koh Phangan, Hat Rin is the place to meet people, especially at the beachside restaurants and saloons along the eastern side of the cape. You might also check out the reclusive scene in the funky hermitages up north on Bottle Beach and Thong Nai Pan Bay.

Out on Koh Tao, you'll get some good tips from the folks operating the bungalows on the tri-isle of Nang Yuan. You might also hang around the **Nang Nuan Bungalow**, which has decent food and beverage service, as well as the restaurants near the pier in Ban Mae Hat.

Night Life One way to get a handle on the Samui Scene is to dip into the night life. This approach is certainly not for everyone, but an occasional foray to some of the after-dinner hot-spots may forge some interesting acquaintances.

In Chaweng, the places to go are the **Reggae Pub** and the **Green Mango Club**, but there's not much happening at either of these places until around midnight, when suddenly people start pouring in from all directions. Both are bars as well as discos, and both serve food late into the night, in case you get hungry from the dancing. It becomes steamy in these tropical discos as the night wears on, and during the 1991 season, certain bibulous parties from Bangkok instituted the "Disco Shower" at the Green Mango. Simply order a brace of ice-cold bottled water from the bar and splash it liberally on yourself and your neighbors. Don't be shy at these places: everyone goes there to have fun and meet people.

Up the road near the **Black Cat** entertainment center, you'll also find a group of alfresco bars where you can chat with fellow travelers as well as local lasses (most of whom, in fact, come from Bangkok).

"Lamai Gulch" also comes alive late at night, but here the crowd is decidedly younger than in Chaweng. The **Flamingo Party House** attracts an exotic menagerie of *farang* and local characters after midnight, and you'll also find some disco action at **Time Spaceadrome** and the **Mix Pub**. For a somewhat more sedate ambiance without deafening high-decibel disco music, you might hoist a few cups of cheer with the gang at **Bauhaus**, **Papa's**, or any of the video bars along the lanes.

If you're in Samui on the night of a full moon, a memorable way to spend it and meet some interesting people is to attend one of the festive full moon parties on Chaweng, Lamai, or out at Hat Rin on Koh Phangan. Ask around some of the popular hangouts such as the Jazz Bar a few days before the moon waxes full in order to find out where the action is each month.

Travel Directory

Hotels, Resorts, and Bungalows

According to current figures from the Tourism Authority of Thailand, there are now 240 hotel, resort, and bungalow operations on Koh Samui, 124 on Koh Phangan, and 24 on Koh Tao, with more sprouting up all the time. Not all of them are listed here. Instead, a selection of reliable facilities is given below, listed according to their locations around the islands, with brief information on rooms, rates, reservations, and other relevant data. Many of the unlisted as well as listed hostels are plain, inexpensive facilities that don't have telephone contacts, but you can still find them easily enough on your own simply by taking a stroll along the beach or cove where they are listed.

The rates given here are based on prices current during the 1991-92 season, but are subject to change from month to month, depending on occupancy. If it's not peak season and the place you pick does not seem to have a full house, you can usually negotiate a discount, especially for long-term stays at the smaller family-run operations.

Koh Samui

Nathon

Sea Side Palace Tel 421-079; 200-500 baht; 25 rooms, fan or a/c; old-fashioned hotel facing the sea near Nathon Pier
Samui Bungalow 50-200 baht; 15 rooms, fan; near Post office
Chao Koh Tel 421-157/214; 250-600 baht; 20 rooms, fan; 1/2 km north of Nathon

Bang Makham Bay

Chalet Tel 421-307; 100-300 baht; 10 rooms, fan; near Garden Home Herbal Health Center

Bang Po Bay

Jariya 200-350 baht; 18 rooms, fan; near Ban Bang Po Village
Sun Beam 250-350 baht; 25 rooms, fan; near Ban Tai

Maenam Beach

Sea Fan Tel & Fax 421-350 BGK Tel 234-6651 Fax 236-7195; 2500-2600 baht; 35 rooms, a/c; large deluxe bungalows with hot water, fridge; small pool, good food

Friendly 60-100 baht; 15 rooms; fan; no frills
Ubon Villa 50-200 baht; 24 rooms, fan; no frills
Moon Hut 150-250 baht; 14 rooms, fan; no frills
Santi Buri Resort Tel and Fax 286-901; 6000 baht; 80 rooms, a/c; fully
    equipped resort; expensive

Bophut Beach

Ziggy Stardust Tel & Fax 421-477, 300-1600 baht 28 rooms, fan or a/c; cosy
    Thai bungalows, simple or deluxe; garden; beach bar; good food; boat
The Lodge 750 baht, 10 rooms, fan; sea view; beach front; boat
Sunny 100-300 baht, 26 rooms, fan
Sala Thai 100-300 baht, 16 rooms, fan

Big Buddha Beach

Sunset Song 150-1500 baht, 24 rooms, fan or a/c
Big Buddha Bungalow 150-250 baht, 17 rooms, fan
Number One 200-300 baht, 10 rooms, fan
Nara Lodge Tel & Fax 421-364 BGK Tel 531-6407 Fax 531-6410; 600-1500
    baht, 45 rooms, fan or a/c; resort facilities
Farn Bay Resort Tel 282-040 Fax 286-267; 600-1500 baht; 80 rooms, fan or
    a/c; resort facilities
Ocean View Resort 300-600 baht; 21 rooms, fan or a/c

Choeng Mon Beach

Imperial Tong Sai Bay Tel 421-451/61 Fax 421-462 BGK Tel 254- 0111 Fax
    254-2077; 4500-6500 baht; 80 rooms, a/c; deluxe bungalows; tennis; pool;
    scenic private beach cove
Boat House Hotel Tel 421-451/61 Fax 421-560 BGK Tel 254-0111 Fax 254-
    2077; 3500-6000 baht; 124 rooms, 34 boat-house suites; pool
Sun Sand Resort Tel & Fax 286-946 BGK Tel 255-4340/4 Fax 253- 6248 950
    baht 33 rooms, fan; quiet cove; sea pool
P.S. Villa 200-400 baht; 14 rooms, fan
Island View 100-200 baht; 15 rooms, fan; friendly family operation; quiet

Yai Noi Bay

Coral Bay Resort Tel. 286-902; 1500-2200 baht 42 rooms; a/c; rate includes
    breakfast
I.K.K. 300-600 baht; 15 rooms, fan or a/c

148

Koh Samui, Koh Phangan and Koh Tao now sport 240 hotel, resort and bungalow operations, something for every taste and pocketbook.

Chaweng Beach

The Village Fax 421-382 BGK Tel 234-0983 Fax 234-0982; 1200-1800 baht; 19 rooms, a/c; cosy cottages; tropical garden; good food

The Princess Village Tel & Fax 421-382 BGK Tel 234-0983 Fax 234-0982; 1,900 baht; 24 rooms, a/c; all rooms are old Thai houses with modern bath; garden

Poppies Fax 421-322 P.O.Box 1 Black cat post office Chaweng; 2500 baht; 24 rooms, a/c; deluxe Thai cottages; landscaped garden and pool; good food; power and sailing boats

The Island Tel 421-288 Fax 421-178; 500-1500 baht; 40 rooms, fan or a/c; beach bar

Munchies Resort Tel & Fax 421-374; 500-1500 baht; 50 rooms, fan or a/c; good food

The White House Fax 421-382 BGK Tel 234-0983 Fax 234-0982; 1200-1800 baht; 12 rooms, fan or a/c; tropical garden

Chaba Samui Resort Tel 421-380; 1400-3200 baht; 16 rooms, a/c; seaside restaurant

Chaweng Regent Tel & Fax 286-910 BGK Tel 418-4066/7 Fax 421-2050; 2500-4500 baht; 68 rooms, a/c; resort facilities

Malibu Resort 150-300 baht; 18 rooms, fan; certified diving school

Imperial Samui Hotel Tel 421-397 BGK Tel 254-0111 Fax 254-2077; 3300-6000 baht; 155 rooms, a/c; hotel; seaside pool
Sunshine Resort Tel & Fax 421-408; 1600-2600 baht; 33 rooms, a/c; resort facilities

Coral Cove and Thong Takhain Bay

Coral Cove Resort 50-200 baht; 20 rooms, fan; good scuba and snorkeling
Coral Cove Chalet Tel 286-953; 250-300 baht; 45 rooms, fan; good scuba and snorkeling
Hi Coral Cove 50-200 baht; 25 rooms, fan; good scuba and snorkeling
Samui Yacht Club Fax 421-378 BGK Tel 319-6042/3 Fax 318-0149; 3300-4300 baht; 42 rooms, a/c; deluxe bungalows with hot-water bath, fridge; private beach and pool; good food

Lamai Beach

The Pavilion Resort Tel & Fax 421-420; 1200-1800 baht; 41 rooms, a/c; 25 deluxe bungalows, 16 hotel rooms, pool seaside restaurant
Casanova's Resort Tel 421-425 BGK Tel 282-0452; 1000-2000 baht; 20 rooms, a/c; shady hillside grove; small pool
Aloha Resort Tel 421-418 Fax 421-419; 350-1700 baht; 37 rooms, fan or a/c; good food
Golden Sand Tel & Fax 421-430 BGK Tel 255-1370; 400-1000 baht; 78 rooms, fan or a/c
Royal Blue Lagoon 650-2300 baht; 27 rooms, fan or a/c; simple or deluxe; pool
Island Spa & Resort Fax 421-178, 421-410; 500-800 baht; 30 rooms, fan; health spa facilities; pool; tennis
Rose Garden Tel 421-410; 200-1200 baht; 18 rooms, fan or a/c
Sun Rise 80-400 baht; 24 rooms, fan
Palm 150-250 baht; 29 rooms, fan; no frills
White Sand 50-100 baht; 32 rooms, fan; no frills
Swiss Chalet 450-900 baht; 13 rooms, fan or a/c; 7 bungalows, 6 seaside rooms

Na Khai Bay & Cape Set

Cosy Resort Tel 272-222 Ex 212 Fax 421-237; 150-250 baht; 11 rooms, fan
Hilton Garden Tel 272-222/213 Fax 421-237; 800-1000 baht; 40 rooms, a/c; large pool
Samui Orchid Resort Tel 272-222 Ex 203 Fax 421-080; 650-1200 baht; 64 rooms, fan or a/c; resort facilities

Nathien Tel 281-430 Ex 061; 650 baht; 8 rooms, fan; quiet
Laem Set Inn Tel 01/725-0267 01/212-2762 BGK Fax 552-5993; 650 2500
baht; 20 rooms, fan or a/c; private cape; small pool; quiet; good food

Bang Kao Bay

Diamond Villa 100-200 baht; 7 rooms, fan; no frills
River Garden 100-200 baht; 10 rooms, fan; no frills

Thong Krut Bay

Thong Krut 100-200 baht; 7 rooms, fan; no frills

Phangka Bay

Sea Gull 100-150 baht; 16 rooms, fan; quiet cove
Pearl Bay 100-150 baht; 8 rooms, fan; quiet cove
Emerald Cove 100-150 baht; 22 rooms, fan; quiet cove

Thong Yang Bay

Coco Cabana 150-250 baht; 20 rooms, fan; tranquil beach; simple cosy huts

Chon Khram Bay

Lipa Lodge 200-450 baht; 34 rooms, fan; nice bar, fair food; quiet setting
Plern Resort Tel 421-083; 600-1200 baht; 20 rooms, fan or a/c

Koh Phangan

As a rule, bungalows less than 100 baht per night have no private bathroom, while those over 100 baht do. Most hostels on Phangan have a choice of
either type.

Thong Sala

Phangan Villa 30-120 baht, 18 rooms
Moonlight 50-80 baht, 12 rooms
Sun Dance 50-100 baht, 15 rooms

Bang Charu Bay

Half Moon 50-120 baht, 16 rooms

Charm Beach 50-120 baht, 15 rooms
Co Co Club 50-100 baht, 13 rooms

Ban Tai & Ban Kai

Golden Beach Resort 50-200 baht, 23 rooms, fan
Lee's Garden 50-200 baht, 25 rooms, fan
Green Peace 40-80 baht, 9 rooms
Boom Cafe 40-80 baht, 16 rooms
Silvery Moon 30-50 baht, 10 rooms

Hat Rin Noi (West Rin Beach)

Palm Beach 30-200 baht, 19 rooms
Rin Beach Resort 30-200 baht, 29 rooms
Light House 80-600 baht, 30 rooms, fan
Rainbow 50-100 baht, 17 rooms
Sun Cliff Resort 60-150 baht, 20 rooms

Hat Rin Nok (East Rin Beach)

Tommy's 50-100 baht, 22 rooms
Hat Rin 80-100 baht, 12 rooms
Sand Castle 60-100 baht, 12 rooms
Paradise 60-350 baht, 50 rooms, fan

Shop around until you find the type of bungalow to meet your needs. Peeked roofs permit hot air to rise and rain to run off quickly.

Palita Lodge 80-200 baht, 28 rooms, fan; good food
Sunrise 60-350 baht, 24 rooms, fan
Serenity Hill 50-200 baht, 30 rooms

Thong Reng Bay

No Name 50-80 baht, 8 rooms

Thong Nai Pan Bay

Panviman Resort Tel 286-900; 200-1200 baht, 50 rooms, fan or a/c
Thong Ta Pan Resort 60-150 baht, 18 rooms
Ping Jun Resort 80-200 baht, 15 rooms
White Sand 60-150 baht, 10 rooms

Bottle Beach (Hat Khuat)

Bottle Beach 40-80 baht, 25 rooms
Sea Love 40-80 baht, 15 rooms
O.D. 40-80 baht, 50 rooms

Cholok Lam Bay

Coral Bay 40-50 baht, 14 rooms
Suan Hin 40-50 baht, 9 rooms
Fanta 50-100 baht, 10 rooms
Wattana Resort 50-100 baht, 10 rooms

Mae Hat Bay

Island View Cabana 100-250 baht, 53 rooms
Mae Hat Bay Resort 50-120 baht, 24 rooms

Salud, Yao, & Son Beach

Hat Yao 50-150 baht, 17 rooms
Sandy Bay 50-80 baht, 20 rooms
Ibiza 50-150 baht, 15 rooms

Chao Pao Bay

Loy Fah 50-300 baht, 25 rooms, fan
Laem Son 50-150 baht, 16 rooms

Sea Flower 50-80 baht, 20 rooms

<u>Wok Tum Bay</u>

Lipstick 30-100 baht, 14 rooms
Tuk 30-50 baht, 15 rooms
Kiet 30-60 baht, 18 rooms
O.K. 30-60 baht, 28 rooms

<u>Nai Wok Bay</u>

Phangan 30-300 baht, 45 rooms, fan
Tranquil Resort 40-200 baht, 11 rooms, fan
Mountain View 70-120 baht, 16 rooms

Tae Nai Island

Tae Nai 150-200 baht, 17 rooms

Koh Tao

As on Koh Phangan, huts under 100 baht generally have no private bath.

<u>Ban Mae Hat</u>

Nuan Nang 50-100 baht, 9 rooms; fair food
Dam 50-80 baht, 25 rooms

<u>Sai Nuan Beach</u>

Sai Thong 50 baht, 18 rooms
Cha 50-80 baht, 15 rooms

<u>Chalok Ban Kao Bay</u>

Tharaporn 40-50 baht, 15 rooms
Laem Khlong 50-80 baht, 12 rooms
Sunset 50 baht, 7 rooms

<u>Thien Ok Bay</u>

Rocky Resort 50-100 baht, 18 rooms
Ta To Lagoon 40-50 baht, 10 rooms

Leuk Bay

Leuk Resort 40-60 baht, 5 rooms

East Coast Bays

Tanote Bay 50 baht, 10 rooms
Laem Thien 50 baht, 7 rooms
Sahat 30 baht, 4 rooms

Mango Bay (Ao Ma Muang)

Mango Bay 30-50 baht, 10 rooms

Nam Tok & Sai Ree Beach

Mahana Bay 50 baht, 9 rooms
C.F.T. 40 baht, 7 rooms
O Chai 50 baht, 10 rooms
Khao 50 baht, 5 rooms

Nang Yuan Island

Nang Yuan 80-200 baht 24 rooms

Thai-style 'fastfood'

Surat Thani

In case you get stuck in Surat Thani en route to or from Koh Samui, you might try one of the following hotels:

Wang Thai Tel 283-020/5; 600-1200 baht, 230 rooms, a/c; pool
Siam Thani Tel 282-167 Fax 282-169; 500-1000 baht, 172 rooms, a/c; good food
Muang Thong Tel 272-960; 150-450 baht, 85 rooms, fan or a/c; night club
Seri Tel & Fax 272-279; 160-300 baht, 35 rooms, fan or a/c

Restaurants on Koh Samui

Chaweng

Wild Orchid Cafe & Kitchen (Chaweng Arcade) Exotic Thai food; gourmet coffees; fancy ice creams
Poppies (Poppies Resort) Gourmet Thai & European cuisine; seafood
Madame Sim's (Central Chaweng) Seafood
Pig Sty (Central Chaweng) Seafood
La Terrasse (Chaweng Arcade) Continental breakfast; seafood dinner
Suan kaew (next to Chaweng Arcade) Thai & European food; seafood
Eden (across from White House) Seafood
Munchies (Munchies Resort) Thai & European food; seafood
The Village (The Village Resort) Thai cuisine; seafood

SURAT THANI

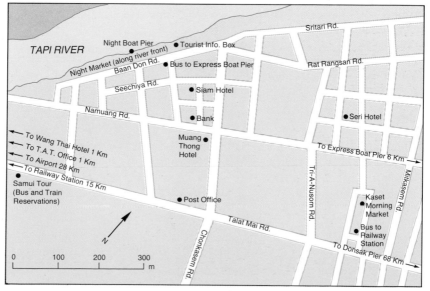

Lamai

Papa's (Central Lamai) European cuisine
Flamingo (Central Lamai) Thai cuisine; seafood
Ciao Pinko (Central Lamai) Italian
Thai Cat (across from Mix Pub) Thai home-style food

Bophut

Tid's (east end of Ban Lamai) Thai cuisine; good seafood
Ziggy Stardust (central Bophut Beach) Thai cuisine; good seafood
Le Bateau (at entrance to Ban Bophut) Belgian/French/Thai food

Maenam

Sea Fan (Sea Fan Resort) Thai & European food; seafood

Nathon

Golden Lion (corner Anthong & Na-Amphoe Rd) Thai & European cuisine;
  coffee; cocktails; ice cream
The Bird in Hand (Na-Amphoe Rd, near Post Office) Sandwiches; salads;
  fruit shakes
International Vegetarian (196 Anthong Rd) Vegetarian cuisine
R.T. Bakery (corner Taweeraj Pakdee & Watana) Sandwiches; pastries;
  gourmet coffees
Nuntha (261/4 Taweeraj Pakdee) Thai & Western cuisine
Koh Kaew (facing sea near Nathon Pier) Thai cuisine; seafood
Ne Nuan (2 km south of Nathon on 4169) Thai cuisine
Sri Pornchai (1/2 km north of Nathon on 4169) Thai & Chinese food; seafood
Samui Food Center (1/2 km south of Nathon on 4169) Thai & Chinese food,
  snacks

South Samui

Phaluang (on 4169 at turn-off to Na Muang Waterfall) Thai cuisine
Laem Set Inn (Laem Set) Thai & Western cuisine

Bars & Discos on Koh Samui

Chaweng

Jazz Bar (Chaweng Arcade) Cocktails; jazz & pop music
The Island (Central Chaweng, north side) Seaside bar; full-moon parties
Reggae Pub & Disco (Central Chaweng) Bar, disco, restaurant
Green Mango Club & Disco (Central Chaweng) Bar, disco, restaurant
Le Must Bar (Chaweng Plaza) Drinks, hostesses
Black Cat (Central Chaweng, north) Thai night club with singers; disco; restaurant
The Village (The Village Resort) Alfresco seaside bar

Lamai

Bauhaus Pub (Central Lamai) Drinks, music, backgammon
Mix Pub (Central Lamai) Bar, disco, snacks
Flamingo Party House (Central Lamai) Disco; patio bar
Time Spaceadrome (Central Lamai) Disco; bar; snacks
Bat Cave (Central Lamai) Disco; outdoor terrace

Travel and Tour Agencies

You won't have any trouble locating travel and tour agencies in Samui. Every major beach on the island has at least a few of them, and Nathon bristles with travel agents offering every sort of service from international flight reservations and tickets to snorkeling trips to Koh Tao. A few of these agencies are listed below:

Songserm Travel: Nathon Pier Tel 282-352 AA Travel 88/6
Taweeraj Pakdee: Nathon Tel 421-126
Samui Holiday Tour: Nathon Pier Tel 421-043 Highway Travel
Taweeraj Pakdee: Nathon Tel 421-285/290
World Express Central Lamai: (near Flamingo) Chao Koh Travel 74
Anthong: Nathon Tel 421-196

Bangkok: If you wish to purchase airline or combination train/bus/ferry or direct bus or high-speed Jumbo Ferry tickets from Bangkok to Koh Samui, without doing the footwork yourself, a reliable and conveniently located travel agency is

Thai Overlander Travel & Tours
390/10 Sukhumvit (between Soi 16 & 18)
Tel 258-9246/7, 258-4778/80 Fax 259-6558

Shopping

There are souvenir and handicraft shops all over the island, and patient shoppers will discover good bargains on many items, especially during off-season months. Listed below are a few convenient places to shop that have particularly nice selections of products, but equally interesting items can often be found much cheaper at little ramshackle stalls off the beaten track.

Mook Rawai: 67/8 Taweeraj Pakdee Nathon. Original silk-screen cotton T-shirts; cotton clothing from northern Thailand; Balinese handicrafts; swim & beachwear

Samui's Silver: 72 Anthong Rd. Nathon. Silver jewelry, ornaments, & utensils

Tonpho: 1/2 km south of Nathon on 4169. Thai handicrafts & local island products

Oriental Gallery: Chaweng Arcade. Silver, textiles, handicrafts, antiques

Hand & Mind: East end of Bophut, across from Tid's. Original design batiks & hand-painted T-shirts; custom orders accepted

Tudor House: Across from The Lodge in Bophut. Lanna silver & textiles from northern Thailand

Fahmui Antiques: On 4171 at Big Buddha Beach. Thai handicrafts & antiques

Shopping Arcade: Big Buddha Temple, Big Buddha Beach

Shop Samui Airport: All sorts of handicrafts, textiles, T-shirts, silver, jewelry, ornaments. Good selection of batiks and coconut shell crafts; also guide books, magazines, & newspapers

Useful Addresses

Tourist Police: Off 4169, 1 km south of Nathon. Tel 421-281

Samui Hospital: Off 4169, on 4172, 2 km south of Nathon. Tel 421-230/2

Post Office: 200 meters north of Nathon Pier

Immigration Office: In lane behind Post Office

Bangkok Airways: 300 meters south of Nathon Pier. Tel 421-358 BGK Tel 253-0414

Koh Samui Intercultural Center: 63, Moo tee 1, Angthong (2 km south of Nathon, near hospital)

Useful Words and Phrases

Like Chinese, Thai is a tonal language, but it has its own alphabet similar to south Indian script. Visitors to Thailand, however, need not worry about the written form, nor even the tones, but learning to speak even a few words and phrases can make a big difference in the way Thais perceive you. It will also help you bargain for better prices in shops, get what you order in restaurants, and make friends with your local hosts. The good-natured laughter that often greets your attempts to express yourself in Thai is not a sign of disrespect but of appreciation and encouragement.

The two sounds you'll hear most often in Thailand are "kap" and "kah," but if you pay attention you'll notice that only men say "kap" and women "kah." These syllables have no particularl meaning in themselves but simply indicate courtesy. A man may add "kap" to the end of any phrase to indicate an attitude of respect, and a woman does the same with "kah." Hence "Sawadee" means "Hello," whereas "Sawadee kap" or "Sawadee kah" is equivalent to "Hello" with a polite intonation.

Geography and Places

island	koh	เกาะ
beach	hat	หาด
bay	ao	อ่าว
cape	laem	แหลม
sea	talae	ทะเล
mountain	kao	เขา
village, house	ban	บ้าน
stone, rock	hin	หิน
river	mae-nam	แม่น้ำ
road	ta-non	ถนน
lane, side road	soi	ซอย
temple	wat	วัด
hotel	rong-ram	โรงแรม
restaurant	rahn-ahan	ร้านอาหาร
airport	sanam-bin	สนามบิน
market	talatt	ตลาด

Greeting and General Conversation

hello, goodbye	sawadee	สวัสดี
how are you?	sabai-dee-roo?	สบายดีหรือ
I'm fine	sabai-dee	สบายดี
fine, comfortable	sabai	สบาย
fun, enjoyable	sanuk	สนุก
good, fine	dee	ดี

not good	my-dee	ไม่ดี
ill, uncomfortable	my-sabai	ไม่สบาย
Mr, Ms	khun (pronounced "koon")	คุณ
you	khun	คุณ
I, me (woman)	chan	ฉัน
I, me (man)	pom	ผม
he, she, it	kao	เขา
go	by	ไป
come	ma	มา
foreigner	farang	ฝรั่ง
woman, girl	poo-ying	ผู้หญิง
man, boy	poo-chai	ผู้ชาย
today	wan-nee	วันนี้
week	ah-teet	อาทิตย์
month	deu-ahn	เดือน
year	pee	ปี
this	nee	นี้
that	nan	นั้น
want	ow	เอา
don't want	my-ow	ไม่เอา
come here	ma-nee	มานี้
go there	py-nan	ไปนั้น
I want this	pom (or chan) ow nee	(ผม, ฉัน) เอานี้

Shopping

how much?	taow-ry?	เท่าไหร่
price	rah-kah	ราคา
discount	lot rah-kah	ลดราคา
expensive	paeng	แพง
big	yai	ใหญ่
small	lek	เล็ก
size	kanat	ขนาด
big (small) size	kanat yai (lek)	ขนาดใหญ่ (เล็ก)
cloth, textiles	pah	ผ้า
one	neung	หนึ่ง
two	song	สอง
three	sahm	สาม
four	see	สี่
five	hah	ห้า
six	hok	หก
seven	jet	เจ็ด
eight	paet	แปด
nine	gao	เก้า

ten	seep	สิบ
hundred	roy	ร้อย
two hundred, etc.	song-roy	สองร้อย
thousand	pahn	พัน

Food and Beverage

food, meal	ah-han	อาหาร
eat (food, meal)	tahn ah-han	ทานอาหาร
prawn, shrimp	goong	กุ้ง
fish	plah	ปลา
vegetable	pahk	ผัก
beef	neu-ah	เนื้อ
pork	moo	หมู
chicken	gai	ไก่
egg	kai	ไข่
rice	kao	ข้าว
coconut	ma-prao	มะพร้าว
mango	ma-muang	มะม่วง
papaya	ma-la-gaw	มะละกอ
banana	kluay	กล้วย
dessert, sweets	kanom	ขนม
fruit	po-la-my	ผลไม้
grilled	yahng	ย่าง
steamed	neung	นึ่ง
water	nam	น้ำ
beer	bee-ah	เบียร์
tea	cha	ชา
coffee	kah-fay	กาแฟ
hungry	hew-kao	หิวข้าว
thirsty	hew-nam	หิวน้ำ
delicious	ah-roy	อร่อย
spicy, "hot"	pet	เผ็ด
bland, not "hot"	my-pet	ไม่เผ็ด
check, bill	check-bin	เช็คบิล

Index